BOND FOR LIFE

BOND FOR LIFE

Jo Wills
Ian Robinson

MITCHELL BEAZLEY

Bond For Life

Jo Wills and Ian Robinson

Published in 2000 by Mitchell Beazley,
an imprint of Octopus Publishing Group Ltd
2–4 Heron Quays, London, E14 4JP

US Edition ISBN 1 84000 413 4
UK Edition ISBN 1 84000 396 0

A CIP catalogue copy of this book is available from the British Library.

Contributing author	Andrea Chee
Commissioning Editors	Vivien Antwi, Rachael Stock
Executive Art Editors	Emma Boys, Kenny Grant
Editor	Chloë Garrow
Designer	Miranda Harvey
Picture research	Helen Stallion
Proofreader	Clare Hacking
Indexer	Diana le Core
Production	Catherine Lay

Printed and bound by Toppan Printing Company, China
Typeset in Bembo

Captions

Page 1	A six-year-old child in a window with her kitten, Argentina.
Page 2	A hunter and his dog from a sixth-century BC Greek vase painting.
Pages 4–5	Two Buddhists take a stroll with their dog outside Angkor Thom temple, Cambodia.
Pages 8–9	A woman stands with her cat in the doorway of her hut in Lesotho, South Africa.
Pages 42–3	A young Inuit finds happiness cuddling her husky puppy, in Manitoba, Canada.

CONTENTS

FOREWORD

Jo Wills and Ian Robinson

Most people have some idea how rewarding the companionship of a pet can be. Fewer are aware, however, of the sheer diversity of the human–pet partnerships that have existed for thousands of years and still flourish today in all corners of the world, in many different human cultures. It is this rich variety that we aim to celebrate in Bond for Life.

In the opening chapter we see how dogs and cats were domesticated from the wolf and the small wildcat respectively. Domestication of the wolf may have started as far back as 100,000 years ago. Tame wolves may have been used to help man with tasks such as hunting but it is likely that rearing wolf cubs as pets or as playmates for children was the start of the incredible human–dog relationship. The domestication of the cat, prompted by its usefulness in destroying vermin, is somewhat more recent, perhaps dating back some 7000 years. Also, since the cat needed no special characteristics, training, or encouragement to chase a mouse, less selection by humans and therefore fewer physical changes took place in the development of the domestic cat compared to the dog.

As the domesticity of these animals increased and trust developed, so began the process by which animals gradually began to take on the status of beloved pets. Just how early this transition began can be gleaned from pictures discovered as far apart as Europe, India, and especially ancient Egypt, where the cat was not just well treated as a household vermin controller but regarded as a sacred animal, worshipped and protected in life and mourned by the household in death.

Nowadays however, for most people the overwhelming majority of cats and dogs remain, first and foremost, friends and companions, often enjoying the status of full family membership. This companionship is so commonplace that it is only relatively recently that studies of the beneficial effects of interacting with pets have been given serious consideration.

In the second chapter we look at some of the benefits pets can provide to people, which can be as wide ranging as health benefits or performing specific services. Dogs have proved

__left__ Cats have been gradually domesticated and assimilated into households throughout the world since 7000 BC.

extremely versatile, providing benefits such as guiding visually impaired people, alerting those with hearing impairments, even warning people with epilepsy of impending seizures, as well as sniffing out illegal drugs or explosives, and searching for missing people.

Pets can also improve the quality of life for many people by acting as a catalyst for communication, providing talking points within families and opportunities for social interaction. Effects such as these have been shown in a wide range of circumstances. For example, pets may assist in child development by helping to build self-esteem, while they have also been shown to reduce the pressence of illnesses among elderly people, and thereby reduce healthcare costs. Unfortunately there are times when people may not be able to own a pet, but such is the value placed on interacting with animals that there are programmes in many countries around the world which allow people in hospitals, nursing homes, or prisons to share in these enriching experiences.

The main body of *Bond for Life* shows the tremendous richness of our relationship with animals in the most effective way possible – by illustration. This section consists of superb photographs from all over the world, complemented by inspiring quotations from diverse sources. We see people and animals working together, playing together, and above all living together, enjoying and benefiting from each other's company. The pictures are arranged thematically by emotion, so that the charming, and often affecting, images of people and their pets are grouped according to the qualities they are demonstrating and the emotions they are inspiring and often sharing. These range from unconditional loyalty and unwavering bravery to playfulness and companionship, from love to sorrow, hope, endurance, and pride.

Thus we see a dog being lowered from a helicopter to rescue avalanche victims, another hunting for survivors in a collapsed building. Other dogs are seen guarding sheep in Patagonia, or sharing the plight of a homeless person on a London street. A sociable cat is taken for a walk on the promenade at Sydney's Bondi Beach; another goes on a shopping trip to an Italian market carried in a shoulder bag, and a lucky cat is shown being rescued from a flood. In one of many touching images we see an exhausted North American firefighter taking comfort from a cuddle with his search dog.

We feel that the presence of pets is one of life's great pleasures and that we are lucky to have been able to live and work with companion animals. WALTHAM, the world's leading authority on pet care and nutrition, has improved

above *Pets can offer companionship, comfort, and acceptance through times of illness, and a strong bond of love can develop.*

understanding of the relationship between people and their pets, and continues to investigate the benefits of pet keeping and promote a greater awareness of the needs of companion animals. Although we now have scientific evidence that pets are good for people, this comes as no surprise to millions of people throughout the world who live with companion animals. Through our work, as we meet both people and their pets or hear about their experiences, we continue to see the great joy and fulfilment that pets bring to our lives.

It is our hope that this exploration of the history and benefits of pet companionship will convey the wonderful richness and diversity of the relationship between people and domestic pets. It is our firm belief that, through the inspiring pictures and quotations, *Bond for Life* will bring the delight of recognition to anyone who has ever had a pet for a friend and experienced that uniquely rewarding bond. We enjoyed creating this book, and hope that you will enjoy this selection of pictures illustrating the sheer wealth of experiences that can be gained from living with companion animals.

THEIR PART IN OUR LIVES

Pet companionship and its EVOLUTION

Throughout history, animals have played a key role in human life – from the earliest times they had a primarily functional role as providers of food, clothing, and transport and, occasionally, as a focus for religious worship. Although this traditional use of animals is still evident around the world today, the role of many animals in society has changed, with an increasing number kept purely for companionship and pleasure.

***above** The dog has been treated kindly in civilizations around the world for centuries, as illustrated in this Pompeian wallpainting from the first century AD.*

Despite this change in emphasis in reasons for keeping animals, pet keeping is not merely a recent phenomenon of the relatively affluent western world. It is also widespread in other cultures and is an ancient activity, older than the domestication of animals for food and transport needs. Dogs and cats are by far the most popular household pets in the western world today, reflecting the almost unique position they appear to hold in human society. Dogs have always served man in a wide variety of ways and performed an increasingly complex range of tasks, while the main role for cats has been the control of vermin – a service that in many cases has become redundant in the modern world, although their role as companions is increasing.

IN THE BEGINNING

The story of the dog and cat can be traced back to the extinction of the dinosaurs, some 70 million years ago. The demise of these great reptiles left a variety of ecological niches unfilled and paved the way for the diversification of mammals to fill the gaps. Primitive meat-eating mammals were already established, but their evolutionary development was slow during the era of the dinosaur. From these ancestral species, two main groups of carnivorous mammal developed and evolved, eventually, into the dog family, or canids, and the cat family, or felids. Among these two families of carnivore, the most successful members were those that ultimately found a niche in the human environment, namely, the domestic dog and cat. These two species have been closely associated with man for thousands of years and their success is marked by the fact that there are few human communities around the world today in which they do not form an integral part.

MAN'S OLDEST FRIEND

Thanks to its unconditional loyalty and affection for humanity, the dog is often credited with the status of "man's best friend" but, in evolutionary terms, it could also be described as "man's oldest friend". Domestication of the dog occurred long before that of any other animal species and was already established by the end of the last Ice Age, some 12,000 years ago. However, man's long and varied association with the ancestor of the dog almost certainly began many thousands of years before that.

There has been much debate as to the ancestral origins of the domestic dog with opinions divided on whether the dog is descended from the wolf, jackal, coyote, or a combination of the three. One popular theory suggests that some breeds of dog were derived from the wolf, whereas others originated, independently, from the jackal. Determining the ancestry of the dog with any certainty is confounded by the fact that there are few significant differences between many canid species in terms of anatomy, behaviour, and genetics. Further complications arise from the fact that the wolf, jackal, coyote, and domestic dog can all, under certain circumstances, interbreed to produce hybrid offspring that are, themselves, capable of reproducing.

Nevertheless, the genetic make-up, behaviour, vocalization, and anatomy of all domestic dogs seem to be directly descended from wolves, despite the great variation in modern day breeds. On the basis of recent genetic studies, it appears that wolves are 20 times more closely related to dogs than they are to their nearest wild relative, the coyote, and some authorities regard the domestic dog as simply another subspecies of the wolf.

What is not clear, however, is whether domestication occurred in a single place from where all dogs subsequently radiated, or whether different wolf populations were tamed in separate events at various locations throughout the world. It seems most likely that wolves were tamed in several different areas, with various subspecies of wolf contributing to the ancestry of the dog.

The small Arabian and Indian wolves may have been the progenitors of dogs originating in western and southern Asia, whereas the small Chinese wolf was probably the ancestor of early Chinese dogs. Dogs in Europe and North America could have derived from the larger European wolf, which inhabited the colder northern regions. However, archaeological evidence suggests that the first domestic dogs were much closer in size to the small Asiatic races of wolf

above *The Australian dingo, depicted here in this rock painting, has been treated with utmost respect by the native Aboriginals since it was brought to Australia thousands of years ago.*

than to the European wolf, suggesting that some movement across the continents, either of the wolf or the dog, occurred somewhere along the line. It is plausible that the domesticated dogs of the Inuit and North American natives may have originated from descendants of the small Chinese wolf that accompanied early human immigrants across the Bering Strait to North America. There can be little doubt though that these early dogs were subsequently interbred with the larger indigenous wolf.

Although there is some archaeological evidence to support these suppositions, they remain purely speculative. Recent genetic studies have failed to link modern domestic dogs to any particular wolf population living today and it is possible that the dog was originally derived from an ancestral wolf population that is now extinct.

The Australian dingo is a descendant of a primitive domestic dog that was probably brought to Australia less than 12,000 years ago by human immigrants of the time. Subsequently, it became feral and has lived wild for thousands of years. Dingoes are thought to be direct descendants of tamed Indian wolves and are closely related to the Indian pariah dogs and the "singing dogs" of New Guinea. These feral dogs are widely regarded as relicts of the dogs that inhabited western and eastern Asia in prehistoric times and give some insight into how these ancient dogs may have looked.

above *Dingoes, such as this one from the Northern Territory in Australia, are thought to be direct descendents of tamed Indian wolves.*

TAMING THE WOLF

It is impossible to know precisely when or how man first tamed the wolf or what its role would have been in primitive human society, but various theories have been put forward. In many areas, both primitive man and wolves were wide-ranging, highly skilled predators that used similar group hunting strategies to kill prey that were considerably larger than themselves. Since they shared hunting territories and competed for prey, it is inevitable that their paths would have frequently overlapped. Wolf bones have been found near those of early prehistoric man at archaeological sites that date back to the Middle Pleistocene period, such as those of Zhoukoudian in Northern China (300,000 years old), Boxgrove in Kent, England (400,000 years old), and the cave of Lazaret near Nice in France (150,000 years old). Individual shelters within the cave of Lazaret each had a wolf skull intentionally placed at its entrance. Although these findings do not explain the nature of the man-wolf relationship at this stage, they do suggest that there was a link of some form.

The transition from wolf to dog would have been a lengthy process that began when man first attempted to tame the wolf. Early man almost certainly killed wolves for their skins and meat but, from time to time, young cubs would have been removed from their den and taken back to the camp. The nurturing instinct, which was already well developed in primitive humans, may have compelled at least the women to feed and care for some of these helpless creatures. Also, some wolves, perhaps those that were least fearful of man, were probably drawn to human encampments by the prospect of edible scraps. Scavenging wolves may also have performed a useful function in keeping the camp clear of detritus and their presence may have been tolerated, or even encouraged by offerings of food. They could even act as an audible alarm that warned of intruders or other predators. Some of the more sociable and placid ones would probably have been spared and kept to amuse the women and children of the group, or to provide extra warmth at night, and a number of these would have been raised to adulthood. Those that did not remain submissive as they matured would have been killed or would have run off, leaving behind the wolves with the greatest propensity for "tameness" and acceptance of the human environment.

Some of these semi-tame wolves would have bred with either wild or other tame wolves and, in time, a founder population of wolves that were habituated to life with man would have been established. Of their offspring, some would have been eaten and some would have returned to the wild but it is likely that humans gave particular care and protection to those with the most suitable temperaments and, perhaps, with physical characteristics that they found most appealing. Favoured individuals would have thrived and reproduced, passing on inheritable qualities to their progeny. By selecting for desirable traits in this way man was, even at this early stage, unconsciously manipulating the breeding population. The process of domestication had begun.

FROM WOLF TO DOG

Some people think that wolves were not tamed for any functional purpose and that they were first kept simply as "pets". This concept is supported by the fact that many hunter-gatherer communities from more recent times showed intense affection for their hunting dogs and other tame animals that had no apparent practical use. These attitudes have been widely reported in such diverse tribal societies as the native Indians of Mexico, North America and the Amazon, the Australian Aborigines, the Onges from the Andaman Islands, the Punan Dyaks of Borneo, the Dorobo of Kenya, and the natives of Polynesia.

Although the young of many different mammalian species may have been captured and occasionally reared in captivity, most of these relationships would have lasted only a short time. Even those that remained tame as adults may not have been suitable for domestication because of a failure to breed

above *The domestic dogs of today are widely believed to be descended from various subspecies of wolf.*

in captivity. Integration into human society was probably more successful for the wolf than for other, more solitary, canid species because the group behaviour of wolves, like that of man, is based on a well-developed social bonding system and a clear dominance hierarchy. Both man and wolf are social creatures, happiest and most successful as part of their group. The transition was also helped by similarities between the two species in methods of non-verbal communication using, for example, body posture and facial expressions. If contact is initiated at an early age, young wolf cubs will readily accept the human community as its pack and humans as more dominant pack members. It is their subordination, eagerness to please, and dependence on man that make it possible to train young wolves, but the behaviour of older animals can only be controlled if these juvenile attributes are retained into adulthood.

The retention of juvenile or even foetal characteristics in the adult appears to be the key to the successful domestication of the wolf and other wild species. Young animals are submissive and non-aggressive, have a low response to stress, seek attention, and rarely fear strangers. Adults that show these characteristics may have a lower chance of survival in the wild, but are perfectly adapted for life in the human environment, where they may be given plenty of attention and be surrounded by people.

In choosing to keep the tamest adult wolves, primitive man was unconsciously selecting for these traits but, combined with changes in the environment, this would have effected their hormonal balance and physical appearance. Domestication of the wolf produced a number of physical changes that are typical of domesticated mammals including a reduction in overall size; changes in coat colour and markings; shortening of the jaw with crowding and, subsequently, shrinking of the teeth; a reduction in brain size and hence, cranial capacity; and the development of a pronounced vertical drop, in front of the forehead. It is the skeletal changes that have helped archaeologists to distinguish between the bones of domesticated dogs and those of its wild forebear, the wolf.

Mutations of coat colour from the wild form seemed to have occurred relatively quickly in, and in correlation with, domestication. The most favoured mutant form was the all-tan, or ochreous, body with a white tip to the tail and white on the muzzle and lower limbs. This is the characteristic colour combination of the dingo, the New Guinea dogs, many pariah dogs, mongrels, and the African Basenji (an ancient breed, relatively unchanged in its modern form). The skins of mummified dogs from ancient Egypt also seem to have a uniform coat colour.

A general reduction in body size is a characteristic feature of domestication and may be related, in part, to dietary restrictions that were imposed in captivity. Changes in the shape of the head and reduction in brain size may have been because various aspects of the behavioural and physical development of the animal were arrested at different stages. Because of the reduced functional capacity of certain areas of the brain, domesticated animals have a lower state of alertness than their wild forebears and may have a different perception of the environment and possibly some changes in their senses, such as hearing and vision.

As domestication progressed, the value of keeping tame wolves in captivity would have become increasingly apparent. Over many generations, those animals that remained closely associated with man became progressively less "wild" in their behaviour and the social bonds between man and wolf strengthened. A mutual understanding developed between them and man learned that he could control the behaviour of these animals and train them to perform useful work to help him in his daily chores and in the hunt. Ultimately these behavioural changes, together with the physical and other changes that accompanied them, lead to the evolution of a new type of animal, the domestic dog.

SPREAD OF THE WORKING DOG

The earliest remains that can be attributed to a domesticated dog have been found at a site in Oberkassel, Germany, and are dated as 14,000 years old. Dog-like bones have also been discovered at a number of different sites around western Asia, including various archaeological sites in Israel, Palestine, and Iraq that date back 12,000 years to the Natufian period of hunter-gatherers. The suggestion that these animals were domesticated is reinforced by the important finding of a stone-covered Palaeolithic tomb at one of these sites, Ein Mallaha in northern Israel, in which an elderly woman was

below *Egyptian noblemen have kept pets for thousands of years, as depicted in this painting from the side of a 3000-year-old coffin.*

buried with one hand cupped over the chest of a puppy. Although it is not clear whether the pup was a dog or a tamed wolf, the young animal was evidently an object of great affection for the woman during life.

These archaeological findings indicate that the domestic dog has existed for at least 14,000 years and that domestication probably took place first in Europe and western Asia. Although the process of domesticating wolves would have begun much earlier, there are no fossil records of any animals that resemble the domestic dog dating back to before this time. Nevertheless, scientific studies suggest that the dog is much older than was previously thought and have led some to believe that the two species began to diverge genetically, if not in physical appearance, at anything from 60,000–100,000 years ago.

From the earliest days of domestication, dogs would have had a utilitarian role. They may have been killed occasionally for their meat and skins but they were also kept for their ability to perform particular tasks, such as hunting, guarding, and herding. Although domesticated dogs were probably treated with respect in primitive societies, there is evidence from the tomb at Ein Mallaha that some at least were also considered companions as early as 12,000 years ago.

The greatest value of the primitive domestic dog was probably in its role as a cooperative hunting partner. Early hunting strategies had involved short-distance attacks with heavy stone axes, but this system was gradually replaced by the use of arrows tipped with tiny stone blades. The efficiency of these long-distance weapons would have been greatly enhanced by dogs that could track down and bring to bay wounded prey, and some authorities believe that the transition to a new and more effective hunting method could not have occurred without this new alliance.

With the development of settled agriculture and the domestication of other livestock that began some 8000 years ago, the working dog would have become increasingly valued in human societies. Dogs could be trained to herd and guard livestock and to protect cultivated crops by driving away intruders. From this period, the dog appears to have become more commonplace with a more or less worldwide distribution, suggesting that they were highly prized and actively traded by neighbouring human groups. Relics of the domestic dog from this era have been found in many different parts of the world including Japan (8000 years old), China (7000 years old), southern Chile (6500–7500 years old), and North America (8500 years old).

above *One of the first uses of the domestic dog for man was in a hunting capacity. Here a dog is part of a hunting scene sculptured on a fourth-century BC Turkish sarcophagus found in a royal cemetery.*

ENTER THE CAT

The early adaptation of wolves to life with humans was achieved because their social behaviour matched that of human society in many different ways. Cats, however, are unlike humans in that they are solitary, territorial hunters that are most active at night. Nevertheless, it was their predatory behaviour that first brought them into contact with the human environment and their strong territorial instincts that ensured their continued presence.

Domestication of the cat occurred much later than that of the dog, and probably not until the development of agriculture that flourished in the "Fertile Crescent" of the Middle East from 7000 BC onwards. The presence of houses, barns, and grain stores provided a new environmental niche that was rapidly exploited by mice and other small mammals, the favoured prey of small wild cats. From early times, a mutually advantageous relationship would have developed in which the benefit to the cat was an abundant food supply, while man was relieved of troublesome rodent pests. It seems likely that initially these wild cats would have been tolerated or even encouraged with scraps of food. Like the wolf, the more docile of these wild cats would have been gradually absorbed into human society and in this way, a founder population of semi-tame cats may have been established.

The domestic cat is almost certainly descended from the small wildcat, which is still found throughout Europe, Africa, and southern Asia. Throughout this wide geographical range, numerous subspecies of the wildcat have evolved as they adapted to local environmental and climatic conditions. These

differ in appearance, ranging from the stocky, short-eared, thick-coated, European wildcat in the north to the more slender, large-eared, long-legged, African wildcat, and the smaller, spotted, Asian wildcat of the south.

It seems most likely that the original ancestor of the domestic cat was the African wildcat, which is only slightly larger than the domestic cat and appears to have a more docile nature than other wildcat subspecies. African wildcats are often found in close proximity to man and are readily tamed to the extent that they are frequently kept as pets by indigenous people across Africa. With the spread of the domesticated form, interbreeding probably took place with local wildcat races that may have contributed to the ancestry of modern domestic cats in different geographical locations. The striped tabby domestic cat in Europe has a coat pattern that combines the characteristics of both the European and African wildcat, whereas the spotted coat of some domestic cats in India suggests an ancestral relationship with the Asian subspecies. Hybrid crosses between domesticated cats and certain other species of wild cat, such as the jungle cat, may have also occasionally occurred, but are unlikely to have made a significant impact on the domestic stock.

Over thousands of generations, many of the typical physical changes associated with domestication occurred in

above *The African wildcat is thought to be the original ancestor of the domestic cat due to its docile nature and its readiness to being tamed.*

the cat as they did in the dog. These include reduction in overall size, shortening of the jaw, reduction in brain size and skull capacity, changes in carriage of the ears and tail, and changes in coat colour and texture. Unlike the dog, however, cats in human societies have remained largely independent and so have been subjected to far less selective pressure for desirable traits. Therefore, the domestic cat has changed little in appearance from its wild ancestors and it can be difficult to distinguish between the two in early archaeological finds.

Remains from cats have been found close to man at various prehistoric sites, such as those from a Neolithic site at Jericho in Israel dating from about 9000 years ago, and those from Harappa in the Indus Valley of Pakistan dating from 4000 years ago. However, it is thought that these were probably from wild cats that were killed for their pelts or, possibly, for meat. Significantly, 8000-year-old remains from both cats and mice have been found on the Mediterranean island of Cyprus, which could only have arrived on the island with human immigrants. Although these cats may not have been fully domesticated, it is possible that they may have been deliberately taken to the island to deal with a plague of mice.

ANCIENT CIVILIZATIONS

Domestication of the cat is widely attributed to the ancient Egyptians who most likely started it about 4000 years ago. One of the most outstanding features of Egyptian social and religious life was their overriding obsession with animals. From the earliest dynasties, animal taming and pet keeping seem to have been among the principal Egyptian leisure activities. It is unlikely that a people who tamed monkeys, baboons, mongooses, crocodiles, lions, and a variety of wild ungulates would have allowed wild cats to escape their attention. And indeed they didn't.

Cats were particularly highly prized by the ancient Egyptians, who would have recognized their value as controllers of vermin, such as rodents, snakes, and other poisonous reptiles. The earliest pictorial representation of cats in Egypt dates from the third millennium BC, but it is difficult to be sure whether these animals were wild or domestic. In the tomb of Ti (an Egyptian nobleman), dating from about 2400 BC, a cat is depicted wearing a collar, suggesting it was either captive or domestic. More convincing cultural evidence of domestic status, dating to approximately 1900 BC, is found in a small tomb at the burial site of Abydos, in Upper Egypt. Here, the skeletons of 17 cats were recovered together with a row of small offering pots thought to contain milk. From about 1600 BC onwards, paintings and effigies of cats, all of which closely resemble the slender African wildcat, became increasingly abundant in Egypt and it is likely that these animals were fully domesticated.

The ancient Egyptians regarded cats, among other animals, as sacred and worshipped them as representatives of various deities. Male cats were associated with the sun god, Ra, and female cats with the fertility goddess, Bast, or Bastet. Thousands of cats were confined in temples for religious purposes and were mummified after death. As a result of their status as sacred objects, cats in captivity would have been well cared for and many cats would have been kept as cult objects or as household pets. Cats were a protected species, and causing the death of a cat, even by accident, was punishable by death. Furthermore, it is said that when a cat died naturally, all members of the household concerned entered full mourning and shaved their eyebrows.

above *The cat has lived in tandem with the nobility for centuries, as depicted in this eighteenth-century Indian miniature.*

left *Not only did the ancient Egyptians keep cats as pets, but they regarded them as sacred objects, often mummifying them after death.*

The Egyptians, with their high regard for cats, restricted the spread and divergence of the species by making their export illegal and even sent special agents to other countries to buy and repatriate cats that had been illicitly smuggled abroad. Despite these precautions, domestic cats gradually spread along trade routes to other countries in the region and were subsequently found in Greece and Libya (500 BC), India (300 BC), and China (200 BC). Appreciation of the cat is shown in Roman, Greek, and Indian art from the Classical period onwards.

Invasion by the Romans and the rise of Christianity may have freed the cat from religious connotations and it is the Romans that are generally held responsible for introducing

above *Pets cats and dogs have been accepted as part of the household for centuries, as depicted in the bottom left corner of this fourteenth-century painting of* The Last Supper *by Pietro Lorenzetti.*

the domestic cat to Europe. Cats arrived in European countries from 200 AD onwards, including Germany where they were highly regarded as pest destroyers. By the tenth century AD, the cat appears to have been widespread, if not common. Subsequently, the cat accompanied human settlers to all areas that were colonized, crossing the Atlantic to North America in the seventeenth century in response to demands from settlers who were dealing with an invasion of rats. The cat's appearance in Australia was probably also related to its usefulness in exterminating vermin and its ability to survive long journeys and harsh conditions on board ship.

Like the cat, in some ancient civilizations representations of dogs may also have had religious or cultural significance, usually in connection with death. In some cases, the deceased were put outside for dogs to consume, as it was thought necessary for the dead person's body to pass through a dog in order for the soul to reach the afterlife. These early associations between dogs and death gradually evolved into beliefs that dogs could ward off or prevent death. In ancient Greece, dogs were kept as co-therapists in healing temples for their perceived ability to cure illness.

Pet keeping by the ruling or noble classes has a long history dating back at least as far as ancient Egyptian times. Murals from this era depict pharaohs keeping companion animals. Greek and Roman nobility were also avid keepers of pets. At times, the affinity of the monarchy for pets provided them with an excuse for incredible displays of extravagance and self-indulgence.

Ancestors of the small Pekinese dog were first bred in the Imperial Palace of China from around 700 AD to look like the spirit lion of Buddha and were kept by many generations of Chinese emperors. In the eleventh century AD, Emperor Ling of the Han Dynasty became so infatuated with his dogs that he invested in each of them the rank of senior court official. Although emperors of the Ming Dynasty banished dogs from court and replaced them with cats, the Pekinese dogs were reinstated at the end of the seventeenth century, when the Ming were ousted, and enjoyed a privileged status for the following 200 years. The dogs were suckled by human wet nurses as puppies and, as adults, were tended to by their own retinue of servants.

In Japan, the seventeenth-century Shogun Tsunayoshi, also known as "Dog Shogun", owned an estimated 100,000 dogs at government expense and fed them on a choice diet of rice and dried fish. He passed a law whereby all dogs must be treated with kindness and spoken to only in polite terms, and decreed the death penalty for anyone who harmed a dog. Born in the Year of the Dog, Tsunayoshi had apparently been influenced by a Buddhist monk who told him he had been a dog in his previous existence. His eccentric tastes are reputed to have caused him to neglect his government.

About 3000–4000 years ago, distinctive types of dog were frequently portrayed in Egyptian works of art and in the art of western Asia. The greyhound type with narrow head, long legs, and light body, was common in ancient Egypt and appears to be one of the most ancient of the foundation breeds. Dogs with short legs were also bred in Egypt and large, heavy dogs of the mastiff type were depicted in Assyrian and Babylonian friezes. These dogs were used as hunting and guard dogs and also appear to have been trained to fight in battle alongside their owners.

The Romans were aware that dogs could be selected and bred to achieve specific types of appearance, ability, and behaviour, and practise led to the development of many types that are prevalent today. Dogs that hunted by scent or by sight, guard dogs, sporting dogs, fighting dogs, shepherd dogs, house dogs, and lap dogs of the Maltese type were common and there were separate descriptive names for each.

As civilizations developed, human-animal relationships became more symbolic and peripheral, encouraging the rise of the view that man had dominion over all animals. Although animals lost much of their religious and cultural significance, some animals remained closely associated with man, albeit subtly, in the role of companion.

THE MIDDLE AGES

In medieval Europe, from the thirteenth to the fifteenth centuries AD, pet keeping was popular among the aristocracy and some senior clergy. Lap dogs were fashionable among the noble ladies whereas male nobility were more inclined to lavish their attention on more "useful" animals, such as hunting hounds and falcons. During this period, hunting was of great importance to the aristocracy as a symbol of power and status. Dog breeds proliferated in Europe as different types of hound were developed for the chase of different quarry. These included deerhounds, wolfhounds, boarhounds, and otterhounds, in addition to greyhounds that chased by sight and other hounds, such as bloodhounds, for tracking by scent.

Although the Bible extolled the virtues of kindness towards animals, pet keeping was, nevertheless, frowned upon by the Christian church of this time, which suggested that the food used for these animals should be given to the poor instead. However, condemnation by the Church was more probably related to fears that close associations with animals were strongly linked to pagan worship. The prejudice against pets reached its height during the Inquisition, where evidence against heretics often included references to close associations with animals.

below *This medieval book illustration demonstrates how the noble ladies of the time were fond of keeping lap dogs for their company.*

Throughout the barbaric witch trials of the sixteenth and seventeenth centuries AD, a large number of innocent people were accused of witchcraft and condemned to death. Possession of an "animal familiar", which was considered to be a symbol of Satan, was used as evidence of their guilt. The accused were invariably impoverished and many were elderly and socially isolated women, suggesting that they kept animals for the benefit of companionship. Any animal could be judged to carry evil spirits, but cats, especially black cats, were most commonly associated with witchcraft and were particularly feared and persecuted. As interest in witchcraft declined, however, the cat returned to favour and even became symbolic of good fortune.

The most likely reason for negative attitudes to companion animals throughout history is that affectionate relationships towards animals were considered immoral and against the natural order of life. Pet keeping was often confined to the privileged elite, who could afford to keep non-working animals and ignore criticism of the practice. However, many of these had little regard for the welfare of the animal. This is because, until relatively recently, there was a commonly held view in the western world that animals lacked feelings and

above *Pet-keeping was fashionable among the aristocracy in medieval Europe, for whom hunting was a popular pastime, as is illustrated in this deer hunt from the French work,* Livre de la Chasse.

right The Morning Walk *by Thomas Gainsborough demonstrates the eighteenth-century attitude that pets were part of the family.*

were created in order to serve humanity. Fortunately this way of thinking did not last.

THE RISE OF PET KEEPING

Pet keeping did not acquire general acceptance in Europe until the end of the seventeenth century and was not common among the middle classes until the late eighteenth century. It has been argued that pet keeping in its present form is a nineteenth-century Victorian invention, when it was perceived as a link with the natural world, which itself was no longer seen as threatening. It also allowed a visible demonstration of man's domination over nature. For example, in the development of new breeds, the breeder assumed an almost godlike role in the search for new variations and the control of animal reproduction. As a result of this new

above *Today pets are widely accepted as a part of our lives. This dog hotel in Japan is one indication of how strong our love can be for them.*

below, right *Some pet dogs are so faithful that they accompany their owners to work, such as this dog beside his owner on a motorcycle.*

fascination with pet keeping, many exotic breeds were imported, such as Pekinese dogs and Siamese cats.

Britain had been a centre for dog breeding since Roman times, and one of the first formal competitive dog shows was held in Newcastle upon Tyne in the United Kingdom in 1859 for the pointer and setter breeds only. Nevertheless, little was known about the inheritance of various characteristics until the naturalist Charles Darwin published *The Origin of the Species* in 1859. From that time, breeding of both dogs and cats became more formalized with the establishment of strict breed standards and it has now become a worldwide commercial enterprise. Currently there are approximately 400 different dog breeds in existence. The British Kennel Club was formed in 1873 and held its first show in the same year at Crystal Palace in London. Similarly, the British National Cat Club was founded in 1887, and ran until the Governing Council of the Cat Fancy superseded it in 1910.

Although cats may have been associated with man for thousands of years, the only functional demands made on them have been in the control of vermin, a behaviour that requires no special training. There has, therefore, been no requirement for intensive selective breeding over the ages since domestication. As the cat spread throughout the world, geographically separated populations may have developed certain features that differentiated them from other cats, as a result of inbreeding within the group and of occasional interbreeding with local wildcat races. In most cases, however, selective breeding, a relatively new phenomenon that has only been popularized within the last 150 years or so, has produced the modern breeds of cat.

Initially, two main cat breed types were recognized, the British or cold climate breeds, which were stocky with short ears and a thick coat, and the foreign breeds, which were more slender with large ears, long limbs, and a short coat. Siamese cats are an ancient breed that originated in Siam, (modern-day Thailand), and were first brought to England at the end of the nineteenth century. It is thought that they were first kept by members of the Siamese royal family. The Abyssinian cat is probably the closest in appearance to the African wildcat, but its origin is uncertain. The breed may have been imported from Abyssinia (modern-day Ethiopia) or it may have been specifically bred in Britain from tabby stock. Nevertheless, its slender appearance suggests a degree of interbreeding with cats of the foreign body type. Angora cats were the oldest longhaired variety of cats in England and were brought from Paris. By 1903 these white cats had been replaced by white, longhaired cats from Persia and other colours were soon added to the breed. Russian Blues, for example, were brought to Britain from north-west Russia by merchant seamen.

The practice of pet keeping in Victorian times also reflected other social attitudes of the time. Pet keeping was not considered appropriate for the lower classes as it was thought to encourage the neglect of other social duties. Pets were therefore defined as an inappropriate luxury for the lower classes who were thought to lack the moral means to control them and the financial means to support them.

PET KEEPING IN MODERN SOCIETY

Present day attitudes to animals vary considerably throughout the world. In India, for example, the cow is a sacred animal that is allowed to wander at will, and its slaughter and consumption are forbidden. In western societies, however, cows are used for their meat, milk, and leather whereas dogs and cats are given many of the privileges of the Indian cows. In contrast, dogs and cats are considered food animals in some parts of the Far East, but even in such communities it is not common for people to kill and eat their own companion animals. In some religious cultures, dogs are regarded as unclean or untouchable whereas in others they form a part of religious worship, and the cat may also be admired.

In Europe, North America, and Australia, over half of all households own at least one pet. In the western world, most owners regard their pets as members of the family – cherished during life and mourned after death. Cats and dogs are capable of forming particularly strong attachments to their human owners and are allowed the freedom of the house and garden, unlike most other domestic animals which are usually caged or tethered.

Today, pets may have a number of functional roles from ornamental to status symbol, as helpers and as companions. Exotic birds and fish may have a purely decorative role and in many parts of southern Europe, songbirds are kept for their ornamental value in cages hanging outside houses. This does not mean, however, that they cannot be considered companions by some people. Some pet animals are also kept as helpers, such as guide dogs for blind people and hearing dogs for deaf people, in an extension of their traditional role as working animals.

Pet keeping is a relatively common hobby in the western world and forms the basis for a variety of leisure activities that range from breeding and showing pedigree dogs and cats to keeping brightly coloured tropical fish or birds as a collection. Where animals are kept as a form of collection, relationships may not be formed with individual animals but rather with some aspect of the species or breed that is divorced from the

above *Dogs are often trained today as invaluable helpers to their owners, such as this hearing dog puppy, which will be trained to alert deaf people to a variety of sounds.*

animal's character. In this way, the animals can be used to make a statement about the owner or can be an instrument through which the owner can interact with other people.

However, the most common reason for pet ownership in western societies is that of companionship. This activity differs from most other forms of animal ownership because of the complex relationship that develops between the pet and its owner. The rewards from keeping animals as companions are derived from the relationship itself and not from any economic or practical benefit. However, this does not exclude the possibility that people who keep animals for other reasons also develop strong attachments to their animals. Pet keeping is a common phenomenon in many societies, including those with a fragile economic base, which suggests that our associations with other species fulfils a need that goes beyond simple economic considerations. That man has had a relationship with animals all over the world for thousands of years is clear evidence that this bond is a strong one.

Pet companionship and its BENEFITS

To millions of people across the world the benefits of living with pets are clear – a friendly face to greet you at the door, company on long evenings alone, and playful antics that brighten the day. Yet studies in recent years have shown that the effects of this complex and rich relationship may far surpass these daily pleasures, from improving our health to supporting child development.

above *Sharing life with a parakeet, such as this one from northern Brazil, gives pleasure to people of all ages, both young and old.*

The unique bond between people and their pets has been shown to improve human relationships, strengthen self-esteem, increase independence, and even reduce blood pressure and blood cholesterol levels. These amazing findings have fuelled interest in using animals specifically for these psychological and physiological benefits.

THE BENEFITS OF PETS

Throughout history pets have provided a whole range of benefits for man, and, as today, pets have been both helpers and companions, as well as simply ornamental or status symbols. Today, however, they are primarily our companions, whether we are walking, reading, working, or just getting on with life. One of our main responsibilities in keeping a pet is to feed it, and while feeding animals provides great pleasure, it also helps us to form a relationship with them. How much of a coincidence can it be that the word "companionship" is derived from the Latin *com*, meaning "together" and *panis*, or "bread" – eating together?

Pets can act as a channel for personal expression. People express their personality in a variety of ways, the clothes they choose, the car they drive and the type of pet they own. The person who chooses a breed of dog seen by society as aggressive may be using that dog as a way of acting out their own hostile or agressive feelings. Likewise, owners of exotic or dangerous pets (such as poisonous snakes and spiders) may be making a statement about their status in a similar manner to the ownership of a rare model of car.

There are various reasons why people develop relationships with animals, perhaps reflecting their personality, attitudes, and experiences. Positive experiences and physical contact between animal and human can help establish a relationship. The species of the animal can also determine the type of bond which forms between it and its owner, as the more similar the social organization and communication systems of the two species, the more likely that each will recognize signals from the other and be able to respond appropriately. This similarity tends to be greater between the more socially developed animals and humans. This explains then, why we are more likely to have a close relationship with a dog or a cat than with a fish or a reptile. Dogs and cats are unique among domestic animals in that they keep their association with man without being caged or tethered, another element explaining their popularity as pets.

Some people who do not own pets perceive them as child substitutes or inferior replacements for human social interaction, suggesting that pet keepers can be thought of as socially or emotionally inadequate. Whilst this view may be true in a few cases, the majority of pet owners are simply people whose pets enhance existing human social relationships. Until recently it was thought that the benefit from pet ownership was confined to the fulfilment of emotional or social needs. Now, though, improvements in general well-being and health are understood to be a common experience for pet keepers.

HISTORICAL EVIDENCE OF BENEFITS

In the last few years there has been increasing interest in the potential health benefits experienced by people who regularly interact with animals. Stories in the press range from children with learning difficulties who have blossomed after swimming with dolphins, to adults whose recovery from a heart attack has been aided by dog ownership. Such stories are usually based on personal accounts rather than facts, but there is an increasing amount of scientific research that supports these observations. Much of this work has been conducted in the last 30 years, but as people have been interacting with animals for thousands of years it is not surprising that there is some evidence for the historical therapeutic use of animals.

One of the first suggestions that dogs aid recovery from illness comes from the work of the ninth-century BC Greek poet, Homer. He mentions Asklepios, the Greek god of healing, whose divine healing power was thought to extend through sacred dogs and serpents to humans. It was believed that a person who was blind in both eyes would recover immediately after being licked by a sacred dog since healing properties were attributed to the dog's tongue. Historically, the Zoroastrian Persians (followers of a pre-Islamic religion from the sixth century BC) also held dogs in high esteem. They believed that if a dog gazed on a dying person this would release the soul into the afterlife. Unsurprisingly, their dogs received respect, protection, and care.

Over 1500 years later, in the ninth century AD, in the town of Gheel in Belgium, animals were introduced to help disabled people. Many Gheel residents provided extended family care to people with disabilities. Although interaction with animals was not the main thrust of their therapeutic approach, they did provide an important animal-assisted therapy.

Another recorded instance of introducing animals into a social therapy setting was in the York Retreat in Yorkshire, England. In the 1790s, the retreat was founded by the Society of Friends to care for patients with a variety of mental illnesses. Patients received care within an environment of love and understanding, which was very different from the many asylums that existed at the time. Some of the treatment at the York Retreat involved animals, with the thought that the patients might learn self-control by caring for the creatures dependent on them. The York Retreat appeared successful and other enterprises emulated some of the new practices.

The important role of pets in therapy has also been observed in nursing settings. In 1859 Florence Nightingale commented in her notes on nursing that a pet was often an

below *Florence Nightingale was one of the first to recognize that pets could be excellent companions for sick people and even aid recovery.*

above *Interactions between a dog and an emotionally disturbed child can often be the first steps towards eventual rehabilitation.*

excellent companion for sick people, especially for long, drawn-out chronic cases. She also noted that a pet bird in a cage is sometimes the only pleasure for an invalid confined to the same room for years. Perhaps ahead of her time in her thinking, Florence Nightingale believed that if a patient could feed and care for an animal, they should be encouraged to do so, to aid their recovery and occupy their mind.

The first use of animals in a United States hospital is believed to have occurred in 1919 at St Elizabeth's Hospital in Washington DC, where dogs were introduced as companions. This medical trial followed observations during World War I in France, where soldiers suffering from shell shock developed friendships with dogs, which gave them comfort and helped them to regain their stability. Animals were used again in the 1940s with veterans from the Second World War, in co-operation with the Red Cross at an Army Air Corps convalescent hospital in New York. Patients convalescing from injuries or recovering from the effects of operational fatigue, were deemed to need a regime of restful activity. An experimental programme was designed to keep their minds active. Patients were encouraged to work at the centre's farm with pigs, cattle, horses, and poultry and to interact with wild animals in the area. The experiment was considered successful, but unfortunately was discontinued.

Modern interest in the benefits of animal interaction is thought largely to come from work conducted in the 1960s by an American psychologist, Dr Boris Levinson. Levinson noted an accidental meeting between his dog and an emotionally disturbed child who would not talk to him directly but did interact with the dog. Further sessions with the dog were the key to the eventual rehabilitation of the child, and Levinson continued successfully to use pets as part of his therapy. He believed that animals functioned as transitional objects, the child first forming a relationship with the pet and then with the therapist. Levinson hypothesized that animals were not a cure, but acted as a social catalyst – initiating and stimulating social contact and providing a route for the discussion of problems.

PETS AND HUMAN HEALTH TODAY

In many ways we treat pets like people. Choosing names, taking care to provide the appropriate food, and feeling a sense of loss when the animal dies indicates that they have an important status. Many people feel uncomfortable admitting that they may talk to their pet on the phone, talk lovingly to them, or allow them to share their bed. Yet because of this, pets unknowingly protect our health and help to sustain our emotional balance. Friends, family, and quality of social life influence our health, and inasmuch as animals act like family and friends, they can improve our health too.

Levinson's early work with animals in therapeutic settings prompted further research both into the role of animals in the therapeutic process and into whether ordinary animals – kept as companions – could have beneficial effects on their owners. Studies have tended to look either for psychological or physiological changes to people whilst interacting with their pet or to compare pet owners with similar people who choose not to own pets.

At about the same time as the therapeutic effect of dogs was being investigated in the United States, a study conducted in the United Kingdom examined the potential benefits of budgerigar ownership for a group of elderly people. It assessed the social and psychological condition of the subjects before and after a budgerigar was provided. After five months the bird owners were found to have improved their attitudes towards other people and gained an improved assessment of their own psychological health. The bird became a focal point for conversation and in one case the presence of the bird increased visits from children, thereby increasing the amount of social contact. For elderly patients in residential homes, the presence of animals may provide them with companionship, and it can also improve companionship with other residents. Such interactions may serve as some compensation if visits from family or friends are not as frequent as desired, although there is evidence to suggest that the presence of animals may also help to make such visits more rewarding.

above *A man hangs his bird cages out on trees in a Beijing park. Pet birds have been shown to improve communication between people.*

below, left *Feeding a dog is just one of the many responsibilities for a pet owner, as well as being an act of caring that gives pleasure and makes the owner feel needed.*

Towards the end of the 1970s, a study of the relationship between pet companionship and health conducted in the United States, showed that pet owners with heart disease were more likely to be alive one year after release from hospital than were non-owners. Only six per cent of pet owners died in the year following their release from hospital compared with 28 per cent of people who did not own pets. The regular exercise dog owners took when walking their dog may have contributed to their improved survival rate. However, it was also found that owners of pets other than dogs were more likely than non-pet owners to survive one year after admission to the coronary care unit. The severity of a heart attack is known to be closely connected to the probability of survival, yet is the degree of severity dependent upon whether the patient owned a pet before the heart attack?

Results from this study showed that pet ownership did not lower the severity of attack, indicating that, because pet owners with heart disease have a greater chance of survival, pets enhance their owner's ability to recover.

The attention, love, and care that we give to living things can be beneficial to our emotional health as well, as it can make us feel needed. Some people feel needed by tending to houseplants or a garden, while other people prefer more direct interaction, and this is where pets can provide benefits. For a child, feeding or grooming an animal may be one of the first interactions he or she makes with the living world, while for elderly people, particularly those who live alone or who are less mobile than they used to be, caring for a companion animal which is able to demonstrate that it loves and needs them can be a significant part of the relationship. It may also be key to the benefits that people derive from ownership.

Talking is an important component of human relationships and, for many people, talking to animals is equally important. Many bird owners are in the unique position that their pets can be trained to talk back to them. Like cats and dogs, many birds can show preferences for known individuals, and will sometimes show affection and "talk to" family members whilst ignoring strangers who visit the household. This behaviour in any pet can strengthen an owner's feeling of being needed, since their pet visibly demonstrates a preference for them over other people it may encounter.

above *Petting an animal, particularly one that you are close to, reduces stress in humans, and lowers blood pressure and heart rate.*

PETS AS STRESS REDUCERS

Following the work on recovery from a heart attack, many people looked for the mechanism behind this beneficial effect, and studies focused on the effect of interacting with a pet on human response to stress. Results have shown that both the presence of pets and interactions with pets can temporarily reduce high blood pressure and feelings of anxiety. Interestingly, an individual's blood pressure is significantly lower when petting a dog with which a bond has been established, compared with petting an unknown dog. This suggests that an animal cannot simply be treated as a drug to be used as required and then discarded, but rather that it is the overall relationship with the animal that is important.

Dr Karen Allen, from the University of New York, United States, has recently examined the relationship between pet ownership and the heart's reaction to stress. As there had been signs that human friends may moderate or prevent a heightened response to a stressful event, Dr Allen was interested in social interaction with pets. Dr Allen recruited dog and cat owners and matched them with groups of non-owners. Following assessment of each participant's resting blood pressure and heart rate, each was subjected to stress in the form of mental arithmetic or a hand placed in iced water. The subject's reaction to stress was assessed when either alone, with their pet (or with a close personal friend if the subject was not a pet owner), with their spouse, or with their spouse and their pet (or friend for non-pet owners).

This study showed that increases in heart rate during the mental arithmetic were significantly lower when a subject's dog or cat was present, than when they were alone. The biggest response to stress occurred when the subjects were in the presence of their spouse! Responses in the presence of a close personal friend in the non-owner group did not mirror those of people with their pets, with the heart rate going up more than when the subjects were alone. When under physical stress, the subjects' heart rates went up most when they were alone. The presence of a cat or dog actually reduced heart rate below resting level and was significantly different from the presence of a friend or spouse.

In a follow-up study Dr Allen examined the effects of acquiring a pet dog on a group of New York City stockbrokers who were suffering from high blood pressure. All the members of the group were willing to acquire a pet dog, but only half of them were asked to become owners, with the other half acting as a control group. Blood pressure and heart rate were measured in all subjects, who were then given drug therapy to help manage their blood pressure. After six months of treatment these measures were taken again, while the subjects were at rest and also while they were performing a stressful task, such as giving a speech or doing mental arithmetic. Measurements of blood pressure taken at rest showed that the drug treatment had reduced it to acceptable levels. However, when the subjects were stressed, the blood pressure and heart rate of the non-pet owners increased nearly to the level seen before drug therapy. The responses of the pet owners to stress were much less than in the non-owner group, suggesting that owning a dog allows people to remain calmer, with a more stable heart rate and blood pressure, during stressful situations. When the group who were non-owners learnt the results of the trial, many went out and bought pets!

Clearly pets help to lower the impact of stressful situations. Sometimes the sight of an animal alone is enough to lower any tension we may be harbouring. Many people appreciate their pets when they come home from work, as the greeting, accompanied by words and touch, can take their mind off the stresses of the day. Touch, which reduces stress, is an important part of the relationship between pets and their owners.

Owning a pet may also protect people from developing coronary heart disease, or at least slow its progression. One study examined risk factors for heart disease among people attending a screening clinic in Melbourne, Australia, and compared the results from pet owners and non-owners. Pet owners were found to have lower blood pressure and blood fat than those without pets. When men and women were examined separately, male pet owners had significantly lower blood pressure and blood cholesterol levels than the non-owners. For women, the only differences were among those who were most vulnerable to coronary heart disease, namely

below *Although people take more exercise when walking their dog, it is thought that other pets may also protect their owners from the risk factors of heart disease, suggesting that some other aspect of pet ownership is helpful.*

those who were over 40 years old. Among women over 40, blood pressure was lower for the pet owners.

Elements of lifestyle that increase the risk of heart disease were also compared, but pet owners did not behave in a consistently more healthy way than non-owners. Therefore, lifestyle differences could not have been the sole cause of the differences in risk factors between the two groups. Nor were differences in either income or socio-economic status found between pet owners and non-owners. Risk factors in dog owners and owners of other pets were compared to see if the exercise taken when walking a dog reduced the chances of pet owners getting heart disease. However, the results showed no differences in blood pressure or blood fat levels between dog owners and owners of pets that didn't require exercising. This indicates that some other factor associated with pet ownership may protect against heart disease. Whether this positive effect can be directly attributed to the pets or an indirect consequence of ownership remains to be discovered.

Although a number of studies have shown that pet owners are more healthy, or at least less stressed, than non-owners, it could be argued that this effect is observed because it is only healthy people who are able to own pets. This hypothesis was addressed to some extent in a study conducted in Cambridge in the United Kingdom. The relationship between pet ownership and human health and well-being was investigated by monitoring the changes in the behaviour and health of a group of adults over a 10-month period, following the acquisition of a new cat or dog. These people were compared with a group of non-pet owners over the same period.

Pet owners showed significant improvements in psychological well-being over the first six months, and dog owners seemed to benefit for the full period of study. Dog owners also increased their feeling of self-esteem, were less anxious about becoming victims of crime, and took more exercise by walking their dog. Both dog and cat owners reported a reduction in minor health problems in the first month after acquiring a pet and this effect was sustained in dog owners until the end of the trial. These results suggested that obtaining and caring for a pet can have a long-lasting positive effect on the owner's health and lifestyle.

Although exercise and diet are crucial to leading a healthy life, keeping a healthy mind is also important. It is known that depression in some people leads them to cease caring and so become susceptible to illness or accidents. There is some evidence to suggest that depressive states can change body chemistry and may encourage the onset of disease. Caring for something, whether for a garden, a person or a pet, can help to protect a person from despair and depression. People are rewarded by feeling needed. Those who cope best with old age are usually those who continue the daily acts of caring – living things such as pets can be especially satisfying.

When life becomes particularly stressful, pet owners seem less inclined to visit their doctor than those without pets. Older people in particular tend to visit the doctor for symptoms stemming from social and psychological reasons, in addition to physical ailments. In a study conducted in Germany, cat and dog owners made 16 per cent fewer annual doctor visits and spent 21 per cent fewer days in hospital than non-owners. The effect was particularly marked for men aged over 65. In an Australian study the same sort of pattern occurred. Among the older age group (54+) use of medication was significantly lower in dog or cat owners. So, it seems that owning a pet can provide emotional stability, which in turn bolsters the body's ability to fight disease.

below *Pets are often considered part of the family. They provide play, build a child's self-esteem, and encourage them to feel empathy for others.*

PETS AS PART OF THE FAMILY

Many people consider their pet to be a member of the family. Family relationships are often complex, with extended families living together in some cases, or single parent families in others. The role of pets may vary in these different circumstances but one common theme seen in many families is the acquisition of a pet because of a belief that it will help the children become more responsible and sociable, as well as develop their character.

Child development is a complex area but social and emotional development are known to be key components and within them a sense of self-esteem is thought to be essential. If there are pets in the house, parents and children frequently share in taking care of the pet, which is particularly important for younger children, where involvement and encouragement help build self-esteem. Playing with a pet can also provide many learning opportunities that are essential to a rounded personality.

One study of school children has shown that their self-esteem increased significantly over a nine-month period of keeping pets in their school classroom. In particular, it was children with originally low self-esteem who showed the greatest improvements. Interacting with and talking to a pet makes people feel good: it relieves tension and makes them feel more comfortable and relaxed.

Another key aspect of children's emotional development is the ability to understand how someone else feels. Some studies have found that children who own pets feel more empathy towards other people. It is possible that by learning to feel compassion for pets, children also feel more empathy towards humans.

Recent research has indicated a range of positive results which come from child interactions with animals, across a range of cultures. Children see pets as providing comfort and companionship, and that they act as a confidant. Pets provide many of the aspects of a relationship that we would expect from people. Pets are even preferred to humans by children for the sharing of secrets or for providing comfort when the child is ill. With an animal, children can close themselves off from the adults' world. For example, if they have been teased at school or told off at home they can retreat, with their pet as a non-judgemental companion and comrade. They can then speak to and feel comforted by their dog or cat, and relieve themselves of their angst, safe in a world of their own. Adolescents can often feel alienated from their parents and peers, unable to share their innermost feelings with anyone else for fear of being corrected or ridiculed. In these cases interaction with a pet can provide a source of comfort, and the antics of the pet can provide a safe topic for conversation.

above *Children can find comfort and consolation in a pet, particularly when they have been scolded or teased by their parents or peers.*

Pets can also help children in more stressful environments. The presence of a dog has been shown to reduce the distress expressed by children undergoing a physical examination. A study that examined pet-owning and non-owning children in a region of Croatia, which had been heavily affected by war, found that girls owning a cat or dog had the lowest levels of post traumatic stress reactions. Similar observations have also been noted in Japan and Australia. Japanese nursery teachers have reported that children who were most familiar with animals showed higher levels of leadership, extroversion, and altruism. Similarly, an Australian programme which introduced cats into elementary school classrooms, found that parents considered that their children enjoyed school more because of the presence of a cat. Teachers also reported that the children's general sense of responsibility and the overall classroom atmosphere had improved.

Children who are withdrawn can gain confidence from pets, who give them the unquestioning love that they need. There are times when all children have a need to have a relationship with something that accepts them for who they are. Some recent studies of children with autism have shown that some children seek out pets for companionship and comfort in ways not shown towards family members. They also seemed to show sensitivity towards the needs of the animal and enjoy touching the animals. However, such observations cannot be generalized to all children with autism, as some actually dislike the presence of animals. Further studies are needed to understand the differing perceptions of interactions and relationships with people or with animals that autistic children may have.

Whilst family pets clearly have an impact on the children themselves, they also support fathers and mothers in their roles as parents. The parents, as well as their children, can receive social support from a family pet, and pet ownership has also been linked to significantly lower blood pressure in mothers and fathers. Pets are almost treated like children by some parents, as they can give and receive the kind of affection that parents exchange with young children.

Although many parents select family pets in the belief that this will benefit their children, some parents choose not to own pets because of concerns about the dangers of pets to a child's health. In recent years there has been interest in the increasing levels of childhood asthma and allergies. Some parents and medics consider pets to be a contributor, if not a cause, of respiratory conditions and various allergies. However, new research from Sweden suggests that the opposite may be true. An assessment of the relationship between exposure to pets in early family life, family size, and allergies found that children exposed to pets during the first year of life had a lower frequency of allergic responses at 7–9 years of age and a lower frequency of asthma when aged 12–13. In school children, the more siblings they had the less likely they were to have asthma or allergies. So, for an only child in particular, pet ownership is likely to be important, not only in helping them to develop socially, but also in reducing their risk of developing respiratory conditions.

WHY PETS ARE GOOD FOR US

Since it is evident that there are health benefits from pet ownership, people have become interested in the possible causes behind these effects, and various theories have been proposed. It is possible that pets have no effect on the health of their owners. Perhaps there is some unknown factor that predisposes people to be healthy and also to be pet owners. However, after a number of investigations this does not seem to be the case, and many studies try to control such factors, for example by choosing both pet owners and non-owners who are matched for key elements of lifestyle and other factors such as socio-economic status and education level. Although some studies have suggested that pet ownership may be beneficial for cardiovascular health, it is possible that these observations could arise if people with the greatest risk of heart disease, perhaps because they had stressful jobs for example, were unable to own pets because of their jobs. However, when a recent study examined a group of pet owners and non-owners, stress-prone people were just as likely to be pet owners as the rest of the population, suggesting that the effect of ownership is a real effect.

above *Many pets provide a talking point for family members, and can bring great joy to those around them.*

left *Pet ownership is said to increase contact with other people, which in turn has a positive impact on health.*

The benefit of pets may be due to some indirect effect of pet ownership, for example where pets facilitate increased contact with people, which in turn has an impact on health. Pet owners have more frequent and satisfying social interactions with people, and a person walking a dog is more likely to have a conversation with other people, especially other dog walkers, than a person walking alone.

Improved health may also occur because owning or interacting with a companion animal has a direct effect on a person's psychological or physical health. A study in the United Kingdom of people whose partner had died examined the influence of supportive relationships (both human and animal) on adjustment to the loss. After three months of bereavement there were significant differences between pet owners and non-owners in physical symptoms, such as crying and inability to sleep, with the pet-owning group reporting fewer symptoms. A similar significant difference was noted after six months of bereavement but after 11 months, differences between the groups had decreased and were insignificant, indicating that all groups were adjusting to their loss. This suggests that pets may provide valuable support during the early stages of bereavement, which is additional to, and independent from, that provided by human relationships. This may be due to the fact that we sometimes talk to our pets as if they were people, which in turn gives us comfort.

Dr Karen Allen has also examined some of the possible mechanisms behind benefits from pets. In a recent study she examined attitudes and responses to stress amongst married couples. Participants kept diaries of all social interactions (with people, and with animals if they were pet owners) for two weeks. Couples were also asked to engage in a discussion on a subject designed to generate some conflict (for example, money or children). Pet owners who had the most interactions with their pet showed the least stress. In touching and talking to animals, people can have a form of dialogue that is intimate, even in public places, but which may not be socially acceptable if it were conducted between people. That the person's face and voice relaxes when petting an animal, and that he or she appears more comfortable and relaxed, is just one indication that such an action helps to relieve stress.

Pet owners tend to have more frequent and satisfying interactions with other people as well as with their pets and it seems that social interaction is a good predictor of the heart's response to psychological stress, as pet owners tend to have a lower response to stressful situations. It certainly seems that talking to animals reduces stress and blood pressure. However, the link between pet ownership and longer-term cardiovascular health still has to be proven.

above *For residents in care homes, animals can increase their quality of life, acting as a social catalyst and encouraging relatives to visit.*

PETS IN THERAPEUTIC PROGRAMMES

The work of Boris Levinson with a socially withdrawn child not only stimulated research into health and pet ownership, but also into the potential uses of animals in therapeutic programmes. Levinson promoted the interaction of companion animals to help medical therapy. His plea for rigorous research was accompanied by caution regarding how to select and train animals for this work.

One of the first evaluations of Levinson's ideas was undertaken in the 1970s in a psychiatric hospital in Ohio, United States. Initially, dogs were kept at the hospital so that their behaviour could be studied, but one negative aspect of the trial was that barking by the dogs elicited complaints from staff members. However, the barking could also be heard by patients, and some patients who had previously refused to communicate with staff, asked if they could play with or look after the dogs that they could hear. Initial experiences of the interactions between patients and the dogs led to an investigation into "pet-facilitated therapy". Patients who had difficulty relating to people were selected and offered the opportunity to form a relationship with a pet. The ultimate hope was that the ability to relate to a pet would extend into their human relationships, and that procedures could be developed for matching dogs with different behavioural characteristics to the specific needs of the patients.

Patients selected for this trial had previously failed to respond favourably to traditional forms of therapy. Of the 30 patients who undertook the initial sessions of pet-facilitated psychotherapy, two did not accept their pets but 28 patients showed some improvement in their condition. Patients who had previously been withdrawn, uncommunicative, and self-centred gradually developed more independence and self-respect as they assumed more responsibility for the care of their dogs. One initial concern with this work was that patients would become attached to their pets to the exclusion of interactions with other people. However, it was found that after initial interactions exclusively with the dog, the dog became a social catalyst on the ward, having a positive effect on other patients who observed the interactions. Although this trial was not controlled, and traditional forms of therapy were used in conjunction with the animal interactions, it strongly suggested a potential health benefit from the presence of animals, since the patients selected had failed to respond to traditional forms of therapy alone.

One of the pet's primary functions in therapeutic settings is to act as a bridge by which therapists can reach patients who are withdrawn and uncommunicative. Some patients, who have been unwilling to approach or talk to a therapist and for whom social contact has been difficult, have an emotional and often joyous reaction that is shown in their facial expression when they are brought into contact with pets. After playing with and talking to an animal many begin to talk to humans again when previously such social contact would have been impossible. Having an animal present can make talking safe, whether directed toward the animal or another person. As animals do not use words, people can safely approach them even when they cannot approach people. Once they have felt close to an animal many feel that it is safe enough for them to communicate with people. Animals are a great help in many such circumstances, often acting in tandem with other therapies. Although they may not always be the answer and may not necessarily produce benefits in every case, animals certainly have their place in therapeutic programmes.

below *Programmes where trained owners take their pets to care homes can bring great delight to the residents and be rewarding for the owners.*

ANIMAL-ASSISTED ACTIVITIES

From the start of the 1980s, health professionals who used animals in therapeutic settings began to make a distinction between the various situations where animals were used. Traditionally, terms such as "pet therapy" or "pet-facilitated therapy", were commonly used, and, although still often used today by the media, they have tended to be replaced by terms such as "animal-assisted activities" and "animal-assisted therapy" which make a distinction between the specific use of animals in the therapeutic settings. Animals selected for use in therapy are increasingly required to meet specific screening and training criteria.

Animal-assisted activities provide opportunities for motivational, educational, recreational, and therapeutic interactions to improve the quality of a person's life. These programmes can be delivered in virtually any setting, and do not require the level of health care and professional involvement seen with animal-assisted therapy programmes. An animal-assisted activity can be either passive or active and does not necessarily have an outcome but may simply give pleasure and enjoyment to the patient.

Passive animal-assisted activities were some of the first to be seen in many countries, often consisting of an aquarium or a small aviary of birds in medical or dental waiting rooms. Watching the fish or birds was thought to calm patients and take their minds off their forthcoming medical appointment. In these settings people do not handle the animals or have a significant interaction, but there can be positive effects from simply having an animal present. For example, in rehabilitation units for geriatric adults, companion birds significantly decrease the depression of older residents.

The animals in these programmes require minimal screening and training – ensuring that the animals are healthy and well cared for is usually all that is required.

Other possible animal-assisted activities that provide excellent motivational and recreational benefits are those that create outdoor bird-feeding stations and gardens that attract butterflies and other animals. Microphones can be set up on outdoor feeders to give less mobile people an opportunity to listen to birdsong. Nursing homes sometimes have a room for observing the birds. This gives residents a place to socialize with other residents, as well as with family members – which is particularly helpful in hospice or Alzheimer's care programmes, where family members may need help in focusing conversations.

Interactive types of animal-assisted activity include residential companion animal programmes or visiting pet programmes. In residential programmes, the animals live at the nursing home, school, or other facility with care provided by staff or residents. Visiting pet programmes allow specially screened and trained owners and their animals to visit patients, who can stroke and play with the pets, at a specific time on a certain date for a fixed period of time. This gives the patients something to look forward to, and means that all those concerned can be confident that the programme is efficiently organized and supervised. Visiting animals may include rabbits, cats, dogs, and other domestic animals, and, although they offer patients only limited access, they are more appropriate in places where care of resident animals would be difficult.

One programme of this sort is the "Pets As Therapy", or PAT, organization in the United Kingdom. Volunteer pet owners take their pets to visit patients in hospitals, hospices, residential homes, and other similar places. Usually dogs, but now including an increasing number of cats, the pets are carefully screened for their good temperament and behaviour before being admitted to the programme. PAT volunteers usually arrange regular visits to the places they go, allowing patients to develop an on-going relationship with the pet. Many pets and their owners find participation in such a programme very rewarding.

Animal-assisted therapy, in contrast to animal-assisted activities, consists of a goal-directed intervention delivered by a health service professional with specialized expertise. The animal is used as an integral part of the treatment process. The results of animal-assisted therapy are perhaps easier to see and measure than animal-assisted activities. The goal of an animal-assisted therapy programme may be to increase desirable behaviour, or to decrease inappropriate behaviour. Animals can promote activity by requiring feeding and walking; they encourage the onset of a sense of security in the patient by their bonding behaviour.

above *Caring for a pet is said to improve life for prisoners, encouraging them to be responsible and express loving care and attention.*

Therapists have used animals for a variety of purposes, from treating clinical problems such as phobias, to teaching new skills such as walking and talking, and increasing appropriate social behaviour. Animals are now used in many therapeutic settings, including prisons, nursing homes, and special needs schools, as well as in individual therapy sessions for people with a variety of disabilities. Encouraging animal ownership in prisons does not necessarily mean that the inmates are ready to re-enter society at the end of their sentence. Rather, that allowing them to care for small animals, whether dog, cat or bird, means that there are fewer fights and improved relationships between inmates and staff. Caring for the animals, preparing their food, building their cages, and learning about their needs direct the prisoners' attention and give them something worthwhile to focus on. The relationships between inmates and animals encourage the need for affection that is absent from prison life. Animals ease and encourage a positive relationship between the caregivers and those receiving care, whether in prisons, nursing homes, or schools, just as they ease communication in everyday life.

SERVICE DOGS

Another area where animals (usually dogs) provide specialist help is when they are trained to assist people with a disability. Dogs trained to help are sometimes called "assistance dogs", although the term "service dogs" is often preferred as the general name for these animals with the phrase "assistance dog" being reserved for a specific type of service dog. By using one title, working dogs can be easily identified in public places, and it also helps to avoid undesired disclosure of a person's medical condition. For example, a person entering a place where dogs may not usually be permitted (such as a restaurant) need only demonstrate that the dog is a service dog and need not reveal the nature of their disability.

There are no records of when the first service dog was trained, but organized efforts to provide dogs capable of guiding blind people began in Germany during World War I. For many years, guide dogs were the only type of service dog seen in many countries but recently, dogs have been found to be equally helpful to people with other types of disabilities. Service dogs may be any breed, size, or colour, and in some cases may not need to wear any identifying equipment, such as a harness, backpack, or special collar or leash. The most important trait that these animals must have is the ability to reliably perform the tasks necessary to meet their owner's needs without being disruptive or destructive. Today, some dogs can be trained to alert their owner to specific sounds such as a doorbell, alarm clock, or fire alarm, or the owner's name being called by another person. These dogs are usually called "hearing dogs" and can provide tremendous benefits to anyone who has a hearing impairment. Guide dogs for blind people not only act as their owner's eyes, but also return them to the world of the sighted by increasing their confidence and by linking them to others who also love dogs. As therapy is curative and the dog does not improve vision or hearing, then dogs that aid blind and deaf people are not strictly therapeutic in themselves. What they can do, however, is act as a sort of extension of the body that can serve a particular function.

In the last 10–15 years dogs have been trained to provide physical help by picking up objects, providing balance or support for owners who have problems with walking, carrying items in backpacks, or opening doors. This group of dogs is usually called "assistance dogs". Whilst "hearing dogs" can be of any size, assistance dogs tend to be larger animals if they are to be used as a walking support or to assist in moving a wheelchair. However, they may be smaller types of dog if, for example, they are mainly required to retrieve a dropped object for a wheelchair-bound owner who has problems with bending from the waist.

above *Assistance dogs are an invaluable help to disabled people, performing tasks such as picking up dropped objects.*

Recently, dogs have been trained to perform a surprising task. Some dogs are able to detect their owner's oncoming epileptic seizure and have been trained to give a barked warning. The person with epilepsy then has time to find a safe place and call for assistance before the seizure begins. Training dogs to conduct this task has been developed since the discovery that some dogs became agitated when their owners were having a seizure, sometimes before the owner was aware of the oncoming seizure. The dogs initially may only make small responses to the impending seizure, but they can be trained to give recognizable signals sometimes up to 40 minutes before the owner is aware of the oncoming seizure. Some dogs can even distinguish between the different forms of seizure that their owner may have. It is easy to see how such a service dog could have a major impact on the lifestyle of someone who has regular but unpredictable seizures.

Many theories as to how the dogs detect seizures have been proposed, from the plausible – that the dog can detect a change in their owner's body odour – to the more extreme, even going as far as speculation that the dog is in telepathic contact with the owner. Perhaps the most likely and simplest explanation is that the dogs simply do what millions of other dogs do – they watch their owner's behaviour. It is interesting to note that those dogs which seem to be able to detect seizures in their owners seem to be alert and reactive animals that have a close relationship with the owner. It is possible therefore that before a seizure some people make subtle, unconscious changes in their behaviour, which their dog has learnt is a signal for such a seizure. Similar associations occur all the time between dogs and their owners. For example, if a person regularly gives their dog a biscuit when they have a cup of coffee, then the dog will usually learn this association, and may become alert as soon as they hear the kettle being filled or switched on.

Service dogs may help their owners in more than simply physical ways. Caring for the animal requires a responsibility that helps a person achieve a more positive mindset. The owners of service dogs and the people they live with have reported physical, psychological, and social benefits. It may also be that the animal diverts attention from the disability, and provides a positive focus for the owners and others.

In one of the few studies of the benefits of service dogs, a group of disabled children visited a busy shopping area both with and without their service dogs. When the dogs were present, the children received more friendly contact from passers-by than they did without their dogs. The presence of the dog seemed to break down the barrier which sometimes exists between people, and perhaps gave people a neutral topic for conversation.

The presence of a service dog can also mean improvements in psychological well-being, self-esteem, and community integration in disabled owners. In another study, 48 people who had each been confined to a wheelchair for at least two years were split into two groups matched for age, sex, and the nature of their disability. One group of 24 were given a trained assistance dog just after the start of the study, whereas the second group acted as a control and had to wait for one year before receiving their trained dog. In both cases, once the subjects had received their dog, there was a significant decrease in the amount of human assistance they required, but no change was noted in the control group while they were waiting for their dogs. At the same time as the need for human assistance was decreasing, self-esteem and psychological well-being increased, and subjects with dogs were better able to stay in employment.

Any person with a disability that significantly affects their life may benefit from a service dog. However, the decision to obtain an animal involves making a lifestyle commitment and must be the potential owner's choice. Service dogs can be either already trained by an established programme, trained by an individual, or can be self-trained with or without assistance. However, it is crucial that the service dog is trained to supply assistance to the person's individual needs, and that the person can integrate the service dog into their lifestyle. Service dog programmes are perhaps most diverse and advanced in the United States, but other countries are beginning to recognize the importance of developing quality service dog programmes and advances are being made in many areas. In many cases, demand for service animals is usually greater than their availability, but hopefully this position will change in the next few years.

PETS IN OUR EVERYDAY LIVES

For the majority of people, their priority is not the value of pets to aid health or as service dogs, but as friends and companions. While society has changed dramatically over this century with the advance of technology and increased

right *Whatever the change in a person's fortunes, such as illness or homelessness, a pet remains their faithful companion throughout.*

urbanization, animals continue to provide a source of comfort and companionship. They are constant in their behaviour towards us and are unaffected by human progress or failure. This can be seen when homeless people are accompanied by their faithful dog who has stayed with them through thick and thin, despite a drastic change in fortune. When people face problems such as unemployment, disease, or the disabilities of age, the pet's continuing affection can help them feel that the essence of the person has not been damaged.

Constancy is also seen in the pet when its owner comes home from work. It makes the same gestures and has the same enthusiasm. There is a sense that one never comes home to an empty house if there is a pet living there. Due to the increasingly busy working lives that many people have, cats have become more and more popular as pets, outnumbering dogs as the animal of choice in many western countries. Independent and capable, cats are well able to adapt themselves to the busy modern lifestyle. Dogs continue to make popular pets, though, and dog owners get great satisfaction when they return home after a tough day to be greeted by a wagging tail.

below *The skills and looks of many pets are displayed at public shows. Here a dog proves his worth to the British Royal Air Force.*

Pet keeping adds varying dimensions to different people's lives. To those who live alone, they may be guardians and protectors; to families they may be friends to the children; to everyone they are catalysts for communication. Pet owners of every age enjoy the benefits of a companion who never condemns, and does not even understand the concept of prejudice. They know that their pet never judges them on their failings. Many people keep pets because they simply can't imagine what their home would be like without them.

ACTIVITIES WITH PETS

Never before have pet owners been participating in such a wide variety of activities with their pets. For many, there is great satisfaction to be gained from taking part in events which strengthen the bond between pet and owner. The traditional activity is, of course, the conformation show. Showing is no longer just the preserve of the cat or dog owner. Pets of all varieties, from budgies to hamsters, participate in shows around the world.

Dogs remain the most popular partners for many activities. Dogs and their keepers can participate in a wide variety of events, from agility to obedience. A wide range of newly discovered activities are drawing an increasingly passionate following, all eager to try their hand at exciting sports such as

above *Dogs can be an indispensable part of a person's job, performing difficult tasks, and in many cases saving people's lives.*

flyball (a form of relay racing for dogs), or the beautiful flamboyance of heelwork to music. Exemption shows – dog shows open to dogs regardless of parentage or registration – have an ever-growing following in the United Kingdom. In many areas there is a reviving interest in dogs which are fit and able to do work for which they were bred, even if that task is no longer necessary. For example, in many countries there are competitions where huskies pull wheeled sledges recreating the activity of sledge-pulling in polar expeditions.

From the earliest times dogs have had a utilitarian role, whether it be in a hunting, herding, or guarding capacity. Although not so popular today, working dogs are still an essential component of many jobs all over the world, whether as sniffer dogs in customs, part of rescue or bomb disposal teams, or working on farms herding either sheep or cattle. They work in partnership with their owner, and often perform delicate or complex tasks that the worker cannot do. In many cases the high level of pressure both dog and owner undergo means that the relationship they build together is immensely strong.

Yet while some animals are bred and reared to perform, most owners are happy to simply play with their pets. Play also succeeds in deepening the bond between owners and their pets, as both are content. Games offer an escape from the complexities and chaos of life, and as we play with pets or watch them in games of their own, it can make us laugh. Laughter, like play, is a natural restorative.

PET LOSS: THE END OF THE RELATIONSHIP

The epitaphs and funeral poems that adorn pet cemeteries express a general hope that there is an afterlife for the animal and some hope of an eventual reunion with them. Many people form immensely strong bonds with their pets and most owners will have to cope with the loss of a pet at some stage – a very sad time for many people. Yet as there is considerable variation in person-pet relationships so there is variation in responses to the loss of that relationship. For some owners, the death of a pet may be a very stressful event and in a small proportion of cases the severity of the stress may be similar to that experienced with the loss of a close human relationship and similar forms of support may be necessary. However, for the general population, the effects of pet loss, although intense at the time, are likely to have a lesser impact, and require a different kind of support.

In most societies there are some generally accepted rituals and behaviour which people use to mark the death of a relative or friend. Unfortunately these are not generally recognized to acknowledge the loss of a pet, but for many people, activities such as burying their pet or commemorating

above *The devotion and loyalty people have for their pets are often expressed in the ways they commemorate their pets' lives.*

their life by planting a tree or making a donation to charity can help to ease their pain and suffering.

Veterinarians and other practice staff can be a valuable first point of contact for owners after the death of a pet. The veterinary profession is becoming increasingly aware of the need to be sympathetic and to make time to discuss the owner's feelings. Although practice staff will only be able to provide sympathy and clarify factual matters surrounding the pet's death, this may be all that is required in many cases. However, people who have intense emotional distress should seek professional help through their family doctor. In some countries, telephone helplines manned by volunteers have been established to help owners with pet loss. Reports from these services suggest that most callers make only one call, implying that they simply felt the need for a listening ear, rather than a need for bereavement counselling or active support.

RESPONSIBILITIES OF PET OWNERSHIP

Changes in attitudes to animals have also made people more aware of their responsibilities towards the pets they own. Indeed, the benefits of pet ownership more than likely derive from the overall package of owning and properly caring for the animal, rather than just its presence. Pet ownership should be seen as a marriage of companionship and responsible ownership. Grooming, training, healthcare, and feeding are an integral part of the package and should be seen as times for rewarding interaction, rather than a series of chores interspersed with more pleasant periods of play and entertainment. It is important for potential pet owners to understand the responsibilities involved with pet ownership before they acquire the animal. In many countries there are also legal responsibilities associated with dog ownership, such as ensuring that the dog wears a collar with an identity tag, keeping it under control in public places, and preventing it from fouling public footpaths. In some countries there is also a legal requirement to ensure that the animal receives appropriate vaccinations.

The responsibilities of dog ownership also include adequate training. The amount of training required will vary depending on the expectations of the owner. For example, if the dog is expected to compete in obedience competitions intensive training would be required, but for the average family pet basic training such as coming when called, sitting on command, and walking quietly at the owner's side, are the minimum requirements.

The legal responsibilities of owning a cat are less demanding than those for a dog although in some countries cats must be vaccinated. Also, cats need little training, other than teaching them the correct places to scratch their claws and defecate. However, for some people, training their cat to perform certain tasks can be a rewarding part of ownership, and cats are adept at learning if given an appropriate reward.

Both cats and dogs require appropriate nutrition, and although many cats will hunt if allowed access outside the home, owners should provide a nutritionally complete diet. Many of the difficulties involved in providing a balanced home-prepared diet for cats and dogs have been removed by pet food manufacturers, and a wide range of complete dry or canned diets is available in most countries.

Responsible pet owners also need to control their pet's reproduction. In some countries, many pet cats are now neutered before they can breed, which can be best for both animal and owner. However, as many female dogs are not neutered, the owner must take responsibility for monitoring its reproductive cycle to prevent unwanted mating. Unplanned puppies or kittens can cause many problems, but even planned reproduction should be carefully considered as it offers many challenges for appropriate nutrition and care.

Successful social relationships develop between animals and their owners when there is a good match between the owner's and the animal's expectations of environment and responsiveness. Someone who does not enjoy outdoor activity or has difficulty in walking, would be unwise to select a very active breed of dog, and owners who are only at home for short periods of time would probably find that a tank full of fish is more appropriate to their lifestyle than a cat or a dog. However, to assist with some of these issues, enterprising individuals provide services to help pet owners look after their animals while they work. In some cities it is possible to find crèches for dogs, where they can be left on the way to work and collected on the return home. In other areas, people provide a dog-walking service while the owner is at work.

While it is not practical for pets to accompany their owners to some jobs, it has been found that people who take their dogs to work tend to be less stressed and more productive. The dogs have been found to be popular with others in the office, and to influence them in their work. In the United Kingdom, the annual Take Your Dog to Work Day is popular amongst some of the dog-owning workforce. As part of this promotion, awards are given each year for the best work- or office-dogs. With working people often spending long hours in the office, this offers the opportunity for them to spend more time with their pet. Despite all these serious considerations which must be made before acquiring a pet, the joy we get from them overrides these by far.

THE FUTURE

Pet ownership clearly has many positive effects, and in recent years, attitudes to companion animals and health have changed. In many countries it is now possible to see resident or visiting animals in hospitals or hospices for elderly or terminally ill people, or in children's wards. Although these therapeutic roles for animals are increasing, the greatest reason for pet ownership is still companionship.

Future research into the mechanisms behind the benefits from pet ownership should allow us to determine who benefits most and why. For most pet owners, however, such research is not critical. Most people choose to own pets just because they enjoy the relationship. Health benefits are simply an added bonus. That pets clearly give so much loving devotion, constant companionship, an attentive eye, and uncritical ear makes them an important part of so many of our lives. Pets provide their owners with companionship, a sense of security, and the opportunity for play as well as relaxation. Animals encourage people to experience bonding, and this, for many people, is a bond for life.

below *In many countries dog-walking services are on offer to allow dog owners to go to work or away on holiday, leaving their pets in good hands.*

A WORLD OF EMOTIONS

the spirit of BRAVERY

Pets can be astonishingly courageous. From saving owners in their homes, to serving with rescue teams who help in disaster situations, they have demonstrated time and again that their loyalty to humankind is unwavering, and fundamental to the relationship between pets and their people.

The German shepherd rescue dog, Byakim, and his owner are part of a French volunteer rescue force, made up of people who offer their services in disaster situations. Training at weekends, these volunteer teams prepare for the unexpected so that they are ready to react the moment they are needed.

"He is your friend, your partner, your defender, your dog. You are his life, his love, his leader. He will be yours, faithful and true, to the last beat of his heart. You owe it to him to be worthy of such devotion."

Anonymous

Soldiers of the Yugoslavian army, with their German shepherd dog, patrol the Yugoslav-Albanian border area in the village of Gorozup near Pritzren, some 40 miles south west of Pristina. The patrols, aided by sniffer dogs, are an effort to prevent Albanian weapons smugglers.

“When an animal has feelings that are delicate and refined, and when they can be further perfected by education, then it becomes worthy of joining human society. To the highest degree the dog has all these qualities that merit human attention.”

Georges-Louis Leclerc, Comte de Buffon, eighteenth-century naturalist

French avalanche rescue teams use dogs to locate skiers in trouble as quickly as possible. Dedicated training is required to prepare the dogs and handlers for this difficult and demanding work. Here, a dog and his human partner are lowered to the snow from a helicopter to begin their search.

SECURITE
CIVILE
DO

"Thrice has this dog saved his little master from death - once from fire, once from flood, once from thieves."

Inscription on the collar of a fossilized dog found in the remains of Pompeii's volcanic eruption of 79 AD

A rescue worker directs his dog in the search for possible survivors in the collapse of a building in a Mexico earthquake. Search dogs are trained to follow the breath scent of living victims, and must learn not to be distracted by the many other smells they encounter in such a scene.

the devotion of LOYALTY

The bond between pet and owner is a great one. Often unwavering in their loyalty, the devotion of pets has made its way into myth and legend, even lasting beyond the death of their owners. That loyalty is all the more valuable to people as it looks beyond the prejudices which can cause conflict among humans. Never considering race, disability, or social status, a pet's loyalty is given without conditions being attached.

A boatman returns to the dock in Positano, Italy. Waiting for him there is his faithful dog. Dogs are well known for waiting patiently for their owner's return, and some people even believe that they are aware of that moment when their owner decides to head for home.

"I talk to him when I'm lonesome like,
and I'm sure he understands.
When he looks at me so attentively,
and gently licks my hands;
Then he rubs his nose on my tailored clothes,
but I never say naught thereat,
For the good Lord knows I can buy more clothes,
but never a friend like that!"

W Dayton Wedgefarth, contemporary poet

Melek places her paw on her owner's foot to remind him to regain his balance during a walk in Pennsylvania, United States. Louis Paulmier, who has Parkinson's disease, is one of a small group of patients in a new programme which pairs Parkinson's sufferers with specially trained dogs. Melek constantly braces her owner to stop him from falling, and can unfreeze him when he stiffens simply by placing her paw on his foot.

“A righteous man cares for the needs of his animal”

Old Testament, Proverbs 12:10

Sasha, the pet dog of parish priest Father Ignatius Fidgeon, lies at his owner's feet during Sunday Mass at St Charles Catholic Church in Johannesburg, South Africa. Sasha shadows her master as he goes about his priestly duties.

"My dogs are my companions, just like my horse and the wind. My dogs - they are my right hand!"

Gaucho proverb

A gaucho with his sheep in Patagonia depends on his sheep-dog to guard his flock and control the sheep in the expanse of the steppe. The gauchos do not train the dogs, but instead rely entirely on their inherent herding and guarding instincts.

the joy of PLAYFULNESS

Pets bring out the child in people of all ages. Play is part of the natural behaviour shown by many animals, with their own species as well as with humans. In play young animals practise those skills which they will need for survival as they get older. Yet domestic animals who have no need of such skills still enjoy play, and it remains one of the fundamental ways in which pets learn to interact with one another and with their owners.

A boy on his bicycle plays with his pet Amazonian parrot in the Amazon River basin, Brazil. These birds make intelligent and sociable pets, and come in a wide variety of species, many of which are endangered by the destruction of their habitat.

“Of course what he most intensely dreams of is being taken out on walks, and the more you are able to indulge him the more he will adore you and the more all the latent beauty of his nature will come out.”

Henry James, nineteenth-century novelist

Two dogs accompany their human companion on an outing in the snow in Chatham, Massachusetts, in the United States. While their master walks on the snow with snowshoes, the dogs revel in the deep snow.

"Life is as dear to a mute creature as it is to man. Just as one wants happiness and fears pain, just as one wants to live and not die, so do other creatures."

His Holiness the Dalai Lama

Tulku Khentrol Lodro Rabsel with his tutor, Lhagyel, play with a friendly bird in their monastery in Nepal. At the age of five, Khentrol decided that it was time for him to join the monastery. The name Tulku means "the child reincarnated" – a child who is believed to be the reincarnation of a senior lama.

64

“Cats will always lie soft.”

Theocritus, third-century BC poet

An Orthodox priest plays with a cat on the Greek island of Amorgos. The priest cares for the cats each morning. In many parts of the world, stray and feral cats are dependent on their instincts and the goodwill of humans for their survival.

“Interaction with a dog is beneficial for humans.”

Buddhist proverb

Young monks in a monastery in Nepal spend a wonderful playtime with Sambu, a Do Khyi. These dogs, probably one of the rarest breeds in the world, were once falsely called Tibetan mastiffs. The Do Khyi are considered to be an important part of Tibetan culture.

“Money will buy you a pretty good dog, but it won’t buy the wag of his tail.”

Anonymous

A boy plays with a Dalmatian dog at a resort in Quintana Roo State, Mexico. Dalmatians were bred as European carriage dogs but, like many other breeds, have evolved as pets in the home around the world.

"Children and dogs are as necessary to the welfare of the country as Wall Street and the railroads."

Harry S Truman,
President of the United States, 1945-1953

Two playmates enjoy relaxing in the sandbox at their home on Long Island, New York. Dogs and children are frequent companions, and can develop highly rewarding relationships, as long as both dog and child are taught to respect each other.

the warmth of
COMPANIONSHIP

Pets and their people have enjoyed each other's company for thousands of years. The simple bond between human and animal has defied explanation, but would seem to be infinitely rewarding for both people and animals. All around the world, people of different cultures have discovered the pleasure of a pet's company. A companion animal is often treated as an important member of the family.

Two Buddhist monks find companionship and happiness with their cats at a monastery near Inlay Lake in Burma's Shan state.

“It is by muteness that a dog becomes for one so utterly beyond value; with him one is at peace, where words play no torturing tricks . . . Those are the moments that I think are precious to a dog – when, with his adoring soul coming through his eyes, he feels that you are really thinking of him.”

John Galsworthy, nineteenth-century novelist and playwright

Two women walk their dogs in Gloucestershire, England. Dog-walking makes a positive contribution to the health and well-being of owners.

"In ancient times cats were worshipped as gods; they have never forgotten this."

Anonymous

A man in Australia takes his pet cat for a walk along the promenade of Sydney's famous Bondi Beach during a sunny summer's day in December.

> “One reason a dog is such a loveable creature is his tail wags instead of his tongue.”
>
> *Anonymous*

Three fishermen and their dog keep each other company at the Malecon waterfront in Havana, Cuba. Dogs enjoy participating in a variety of activities with their human partners, always keen to accompany their owners.

“The smallest feline is a masterpiece.”

Leonardo da Vinci, fifteenth-century painter, sculptor, architect, engineer, and scientist.

A shopper in Milan, Italy, enjoys the sights and sounds of a market. The cat accompanies his owner on this trip, observing the activity from the safety of a shoulder-bag.

> "The greatness of a nation and its moral progress can be judged by the way its animals are treated."
>
> *Mahatma Gandhi, twentieth-century Indian political and spiritual leader*

An Indian family share their breakfast with their cat. Around the world, people share their lives and possessions with pets, considering the rewards they receive in return to be ample payment for their generosity.

"A bird does not sing because it has an answer. It sings because it has a song."

Chinese proverb

In China, elderly men bring their pet birds for singing practise outside the walls of Xian. All across the Far East, singing birds are prized as companions. Kept in decorative cages, their owners take them for walks and visit restaurants and gathering places where they can keep company with other bird owners.

> "Dogs are not only a product of their own temperament, but of their owner's as well. You never really train a dog so much as train the owner."
>
> *Anonymous*

An Islamic soldier prepares food for a dog at a position in the Botlikh region of Dagestan in southern Russia. Dogs are well known for their willingness to stay with their human companions in difficult situations.

"The view looks the same to every dog, but the lead dog."

Inuit proverb

A Canadian Inuit shares a rest with his husky in Churchill-Hudson Bay, Canada, with his furs and the dog's thick coat protecting both from the cold. For those who live on the ice, these hardy dogs are vital to survival.

the power of LOVE

People share a great deal of love and compassion with their pets. Owners, and even complete strangers, go to great lengths to be there when pets need help. Just as often, however, it is the pets who are there to support their owners. Pets have the ability to make people feel loved through their constant and unquestioning devotion.

Carl, seen here with his dog, Oi, on a bus in England, used to be homeless. Oi has been his constant companion during his struggle to make a home for himself. Now happily settled, and with a family of his own, Carl still enjoys spending time with his friend.

“Dog. A kind of additional or subsidiary Deity designed to catch the overflow and surplus of the world's worship.”

Ambrose Bierce, nineteenth-century writer and journalist

Roger Haines hugs his dog, Sebastina, after she spent five days in the rubble left by an Oklahoma tornado in the United States. Sebastina had been buried in a washing machine since the tornado destroyed the neighbourhood.

"He that denies the cat skimmed milk must give the mouse cream."

Russian proverb

A man sits on the ice of a Moscow river as he tries to catch fish for his pet cat. Ice-fishing is a traditional winter pastime in Russia.

"Why people should prefer a wet cat to a dry one I have never been able to understand; but that a wet cat is practically sure of being taken in and gushed over, while a dry cat is liable to have the garden hose turned upon it, is an undoubted fact."

Jerome K Jerome, nineteenth-century actor and author

Lawrence Katz carries his cat down a flooded street in West Des Moines, Iowa, in the United States. Animals often need a helping hand when disaster overtakes their environment.

PAWS
SERVICE DOG

"The one absolutely unselfish friend that man can have in this selfish world, the one that never deserts him, the one that never moves ungrateful or treacherous, is his dog. He will kiss the hand that has no food to offer. When all other friends desert, he remains."

George G Vest, senator of Missouri,
United States, 1879-1903

Lane Phalen takes time out to give her service dog, Beau, a cuddle in the kitchen of her Illinois home in the United States. Phalen, who has multiple sclerosis, is one of thousands of people using service dogs to help with everyday activities made difficult by disabilities.

"The earth trembled and a great rift appeared, separating the first man and woman from the rest of the animal kingdom. As the chasm grew deeper and wider, all the other creatures, afraid for their lives, returned to the forest – except for the dog who, after much consideration, leapt the perilous rift to stay with the humans on the other side. His love for humanity was greater than his bond to other creatures, he explained, and he willingly forfeited his place in paradise to prove it."

Native American folktale, Ojibway tribe

Firefighter Skip Fernandez of Miami, Florida, takes comfort in the company of his search dog, Aspen, after an exhausting 12-hour-long shift searching for survivors in the wreckage of the Federal Building following the Oklahoma City bombing in April 1995. Search dogs and their handlers played a vital part in the rescue effort.

RESCUE

> “Every life should have nine cats.”
>
> *Anonymous*

A rescue worker shows compassion to a cat saved from a devastated apartment building in the Russian city of Volgodonsk, near the volatile and mountainous Caucasus region. A suspected bomb devastated the apartment building resulting in numerous casualties.

the weight of SORROW

Sorrow can be made easier to bear by sharing it with the gentle compassion of a concerned pet. However, pet owners also know that one day they will have to face the sorrow of the loss of that pet. Such a loss can be hard to bear, but is often softened by happy memories of that special friend.

Seeking their lost dog, two children put up a poster on a telegraph pole in their home state of Florida in the United States. For the many dogs who stray each year, life is uncertain in spite of rescue work and shelters for homeless dogs.

Perdido
"Tribilin"
LLAMAR
4487667
RECOMPENSA

“One reason a dog is such a comfort when you’re downcast is that he doesn’t ask to know why.”

Anonymous

A dog waits patiently while his owner visits the grave of a loved one in a cemetery in Saint Tropez, France.

HOMELESS
+
HUNGRY
PLEASE HELP
THANK you

"I, who had had my heart full for hours, took advantage of an early moment of solitude, to cry in it very bitterly. Suddenly a little hairy head thrust itself from behind my pillow into my face, rubbing its ears and nose against me in a responsive agitation, and drying the tears as they came."

Elizabeth Barrett Browning, nineteenth-century poet and author

A homeless young person begs on London's Embankment, accompanied by a faithful dog. Many of the homeless make sure their dogs are well cared-for in spite of their meagre resources. In exchange, they get companionship and consideration.

ICHAUWAY'S
SWEET BREEZE
A GALLANT LADY
HER COURSE IS RUN
1948
C. D.
ICHAUWAY'S WOOF
1930 — 1941

“I think God will have prepared everything for our perfect happiness (in Heaven). If it takes my dog being there, I believe he’ll be there.”

Reverend Billy Graham, contemporary evangelist

The important role pets play in the lives of their owners often makes them part of the family, and when a cherished pet dies the grief can be intense. This dog cemetery in Georgia, United States, gives owners a place to remember their pets.

the strength of HOPE

The relationship between pets and people provides hope for many. In some cases, the animals may play an active role in the future of their owners. In others, they provide reassurance and optimism simply by their presence. Even a simple cuddle with a warm bundle of fur can make a huge difference in some people's lives.

A dachshund puppy from a shelter gives enormous pleasure to a patient from a nursing home in New York. As pets often encourage positive emotions and reactions in people they are becoming increasingly popular in therapeutic programmes.

“If there are no dogs in Heaven, then when I die I want to go where they went.”

Anonymous

Father Jorge Christopherson performs the blessing of the animals for a group of dogs outside the San Francisco Church in Lima, Peru. Animal blessing takes place at churches in many parts of the world.

SAN JORGE

From a cat: “Then my Man lifts me up and buries his warm face in my fur. Just then, for a second a flash of higher existence awakens him, and he sighs with bliss and purrs something which is almost understandable.”

Karel Capek, twentieth-century Czech novelist

A Bosnian Serb refugee boy clings tightly to his cat, hoping for a safe future, while waiting for transportation in the Sarajevo suburb of Ilijas. Pets often provide comfort to children in times of trouble and anxiety.

the determination of
ENDURANCE

The endurance of pet animals is often astonishing. From travelling great distances to surviving danger, pets have the ability to endure much side by side with their people. The power of the partnership is strong enough to drive a pet to search far and wide for their owner when they are lost, and to survive conditions far beyond those to which they are accustomed.

Blind hiker William Irwin is guided by his pet dog on his extraordinary journey from Georgia to Maine in the United States, a trek of over 2000 miles.

“Humankind is drawn to dogs because they are so like ourselves – bumbling, affectionate, confused, easily disappointed, eager to be amused, grateful for kindness and the least attention.”

Pam Brown, contemporary New Zealand poet

A skier and his Labrador set off through the blowing snow at the Lewis Pass, South Island, New Zealand. Many dogs enjoy activities in the snow, and most enjoy having adventures with their owners.

“Lord, I keep watch! If I am not here who will guard their house, watch over their sheep, be faithful? No one but You and I understand what faithfulness is. They call me ‘Good Dog! Nice Dog !’ Words...”

Anonymous

An unusual sight for this part of the world, motorcycle-riding Caroline Fenton introduced her Australian kelpies to Patagonia as herding dogs to work on a vast area of land. To accompany Caroline in her work they ride alongside her on her motorbike to reach the sheep they have to herd.

"His puppyhood was a period of foolish rebellion. He was always worsted, but he fought back because it was his nature to fight back. And he was unconquerable."

Jack London, nineteenth-century author

A group of Inuit hunters watch their sure-footed huskies pick their way ashore over the thin, new sea ice in Greenland.

"The more I see of the representatives of the people, the more I admire my dogs."

Alphonse de Lamartine, nineteenth-century poet and author

Here a French rescue dog works with his avalanche team. Dogs play a vital role in saving mountaineers and skiers in difficulty. After an avalanche, the arrival of a dog on the scene can make the difference between life and death for a missing skier.

POLICE

the dignity of PRIDE

All over the world, people take great pride in their pets. From formal occasions to walks in the park, owners love to show off their animals. Responsive to attention, pets thrive on the approval of their owners and enjoy participating in many different types of event with their people.

A tribal hunter with his dog in a forest near M'Lomp village in Casamance, Senegal. Hunting dogs the world over have long been a source of pride for their owners, who boast of their skills in the field.

"To call him a dog hardly seems to do him justice, although inasmuch as he had four legs and a tail and barked, I admit he was, to all outward appearances. But to those of us who knew him well, he was a perfect gentleman."

Hermione Gingold, twentieth-century actress

Kirby the papillon and his owner John Oulton celebrate their win at the Westminster dog show in Madison Square Garden, New York. Otherwise known as Champion Loteki Supernatural Being, Kirby won America's premier dog show in 1999.

BEST
IN
SHOW

“The Arab loves the horse, the falcon and the dog, the saluki.”

Sheik Mohammad bin Rashid al-Maktoum, crown prince of Dubai

A man in Al Ain, Abu Dhabi, hunts with his falcon in the desert. Originally the desert bedouin's only way to hunt fresh wild meat, falconry is an important part of Gulf Arab culture and a popular sport.

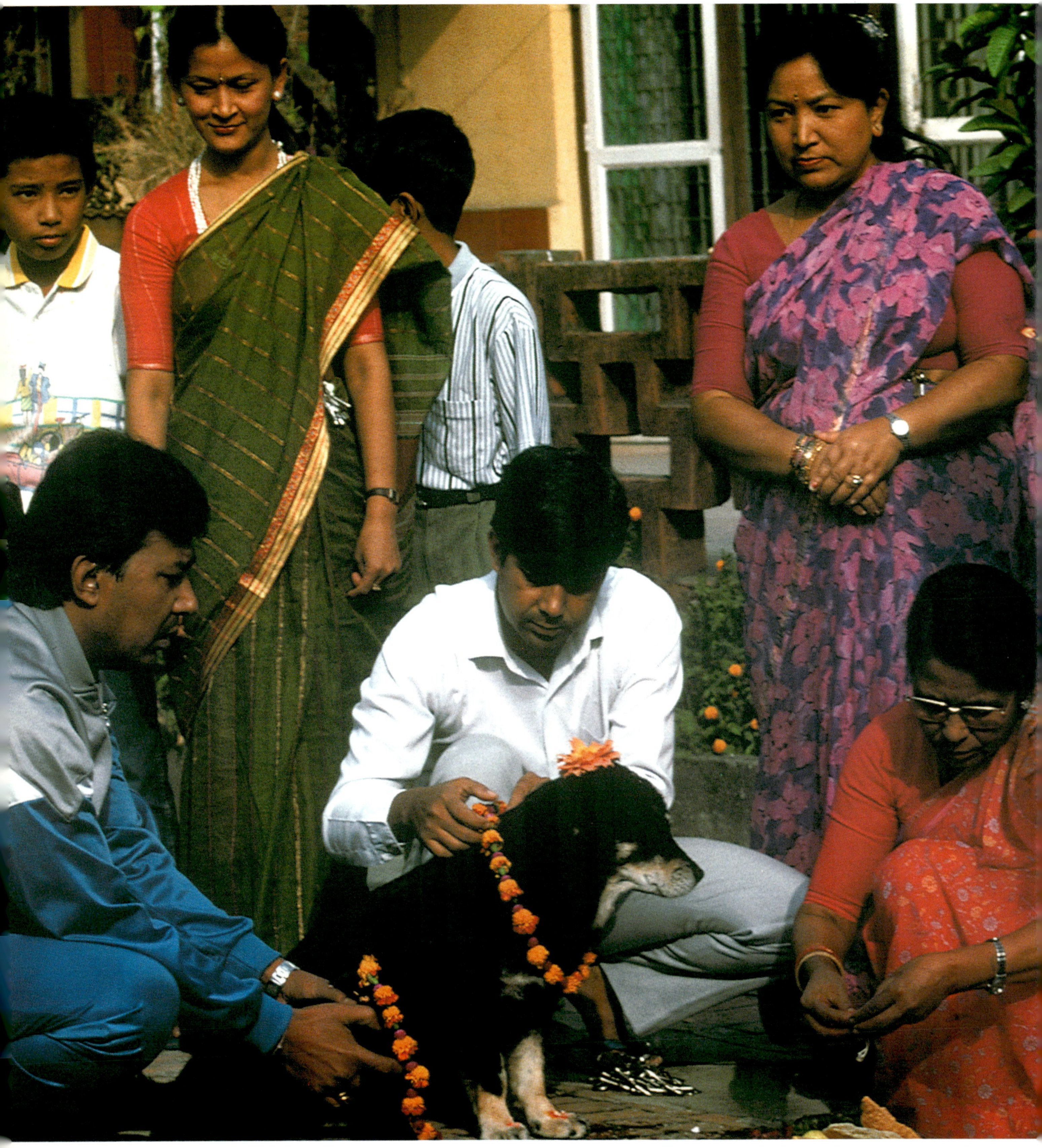

> “Like the body that is made up of different limbs and organs, all mortal creatures exist depending upon one another.”
>
> *Hindu proverb*

On one day a year, dogs are celebrated by Hindus in the festival of dogs, Kukur Tihar. The dogs are decorated with wreaths, flowers, and the tika – the typical Hindu mark on the forehead – as seen here in Kathmandu, Nepal. The dogs are honoured in the family as the guardians of the dead.

"Recollect that the Almighty,
who gave the dog to be
companion of our pleasure
and our toils, hath invested
him with a nature noble
and incapable of deceit."

Sir Walter Scott, nineteenth-century novelist and poet

Dave Myers, Community Fire Safety Officer for Northumberland, United Kingdom, shows off his fire and rescue dog. The dog was presented with a WAG Award (Willing And Giving Award) by the Animal Health Trust in 1999.

“There is only one smartest dog in the world, and everybody has it.”

Anonymous

A Gumbiano Indian boy stands proudly with his mongrel farm dog at a funeral in Cauca, Columbia.

“An Indian and a dog never get lost.”

Central American proverb

A policeman and his dog take part in an annual festival of flowers in Columbia. Within the region this kind of partnership is seldom seen, as it is not common for the police in the area to work with dogs.

INDEX

PICTURE CREDITS

1 Britstock IFA/Pedro L Raota; 2 AKG, London; 4-5 Bruno Barbey/Magnum; 6 AKG, London/Jean-Louis Nou; 7 Corbis UK Ltd/Tom Nebbia; 8-9 Getty One Stone/Nicholas DeVore; 10 AKG, London/Erich Lessing; 11 Lochman Transparencies/Wade Hughes; 12 NHPA/A Warburton & S Toon; 13 NHPA/Andy Rouse; 14 Associated Press Ltd/Enric Marti; 15 Sonia Halliday Photographs; 16 NHPA/Nigel J Dennis; 17 top right AKG, London/Jean-Louis Nou; 17 bottom left Ancient Art and Architecture Collection; 18 Sonia Halliday Photographs; 19 AKG, London; 20 AKG, London; 21 AISA/National Gallery, London; 22 top Chris Steele-Perkins/Magnum Photos; 22 bottom Photonica/T Taniguchi; 23 Hearing Dogs For Deaf People; 24 Bruce Coleman Ltd/Luiz Claudio Marigo; 25 AKG, London; 26 Mary Bloom; 27 top Getty One Stone/Keren Su; 27 bottom RSPCA/Angela Hampton; 28 Image Bank; 29 Marc Henrie; 30 RSPCA/Klaus-Peter Wolf; 31 The Stock Market/Chris Jones; 32 top Jo Wills; 32 bottom Richard Kalvar/Magnum; 33 Marc Henrie; 34 Animal Photography/Sally Anne Thompson; 35 English Heritage/Crown Copyright NMR; 36 Marc Henrie; 37 RSPCA/Andrew Forsyth; 38 Marc Henrie; 39 FLPA/Gerard Laci; 40 Colorific/Manfred Horvath/Anzenberger; 41 Frank Spooner Pictures Ltd/Ferry/Liaison; 42-43 World Pictures; 45 FLPA; 46 Associated Press Ltd; 48-49 Frank Spooner Pictures Ltd/Bosio; 50-51 Camera Press/Benoit Gysembergh; 53 Axiom Photographic Agency/Lucy Davies; 54 Associated Press Ltd; 56-57 Associated Press Ltd/Denis Farrell; 58-59 TopTV Produktion Gmbh; 61 National Geographic Image Collection/Blair James; 62-63 The Stock Market/Michael Kevin Daly; 64-65 Martine Franck/Magnum; 66-67 Network/Rapho/Hans Silvester; 68-69 TopTV Produktion Gmbh; 70-71 National Geographic Image Collection/Tomasz Tomaszewski; 72-73 Mary Bloom; 75 Getty One Stone; 77 Animal Photography/R Wilbie; 78-79 Popperfoto/Reuters/Megan Lewis; 80-81 Frank Spooner Pictures Ltd/Gamma Liaison/Ferry; 82-83 Ferdinando Scianna/Magnum; 84-85 Panos Pictures/Liba Taylor; 86-87 Ian Berry/Magnum; 88-89 Associated Press AP/Ruslan Musayev; 90-91 World Pictures; 93 Panos Pictures; 94 Associated Press Ltd/J Pat Carter; 96 Associated Press Ltd; 98-99 Associated Press Ltd/John Gaps; 100 Associated Press Ltd/Beth Kaiser; 103 Associated Press Ltd; 104-105 Associated Press Ltd; 107 The Stock Market; 108-109 Elliott Erwitt/Magnum Photos; 110 Panos Pictures/Mark McEvoy; 112-113 Danny Lyon/Magnum Photos; 115 Mary Bloom; 117 Associated Press Ltd; 118 Associated Press Ltd; 121 National Geographic Image Collection/Lauren Greenfield; 122-123 Hedgehog House/Colin Monteath; 124-125 TopTV Produktion Gmbh; 126-127 Bryan & Cherry Alexander; 128-129 Frank Spooner Pictures Ltd/Gamma/Bosio; 131 Rene Burri/ Magnum Photos; 133 Associated Press Ltd/Mark Lennihan; 134-135 Impact/Caroline Penn; 136-137 TopTV Produktion Gmbh; 138 Animal Health Trust; 140-141 Panos Pictures/Jeremy Horner; 142 Panos Pictures/Jon Spall.